D1611396

THE BIRTH, THE CURSE AND THE GREENING OF EARTH

The Earth Bible Commentary Series, 1

Series Editor
Norman Habel

Dedicated to
Wilhelm Gottfried Habel
my great grandfather,
an early environmentalist
on a farm in Victoria, Australia,
in the 19th century.

THE BIRTH, THE CURSE AND THE GREENING OF EARTH

AN ECOLOGICAL READING OF GENESIS 1–11

Norman Habel

SHEFFIELD PHOENIX PRESS

2011

Copyright © 2011 Sheffield Phoenix Press

Published by Sheffield Phoenix Press
Department of Biblical Studies, University of Sheffield,
45 Victoria Street, Sheffield S3 7QB
UK

www.sheffieldphoenix.com

A CIP catalogue record for this book
is available from the British Library

Typeset by ISB Typesetting
Printed on acid-free paper by Lightning Source UK Ltd, Milton Keynes

ISBN 978-1-907534-19-5 (hardback)

CONTENTS

Terminology

Adam—the human/human being, derived from *Adamah*, as distinct from Adam, the name given to the first human in the Genesis genealogies

Adamah—the fertile ground; the central domain/character in the *Adamah* myth

Adamah myth—a sequence or cycle of origin stories set in the primordial in which *Adamah* is the central domain/character

basar—flesh; the term for all life in the *Erets* myth

Elohim—God and the name of God used in the *Erets* myth

Erets—Earth, as distinct from sky (*shamayim*); the central domain/character in the *Erets* myth

Erets myth—a sequence or cycle of origin stories set in the primordial in which *Erets* is the central domain/character

Yhwh—the four consonants designating the name of Israel's God; the name for God in the *Adamah* myth

shamayim—sky, as distinct from heaven; the domain/character in the *Erets* myth from which *Erets* is separated

toledoth—generations; the designation used as a framing device for the collected myths and legends in Genesis 1–11

tselem—image, concrete replica; a central symbol in the *Tselem* myth

Tselem myth—a sequence of origin stories, some only fragments, set in the primordial in which *tselem* is the central symbol

Note on transliteration: where *Adam*, *Adamah*, and *Erets* function as central figures in a given myth, the silent aleph at the beginning of the word is deleted to facilitate reading; the definite article is also omitted to highlight that these figures are characters/domains of the myth rather than background scenery.

In 1964 I wrote my first major paper on Genesis 2–3 for an assembly of the Lutheran hierarchy in St Louis. I was accused of heresy by some for daring to suggest that this Genesis narrative may be 'more than history'. Over the years, I have applied a wide range of critical approaches to Genesis 1–11. In this volume, I am suggesting that if we read Genesis employing an ecological hermeneutics, we discover new dimensions of meaning. Of course, Genesis 1–11 embraces several myths. Perhaps today, as we read with ecological eyes, we may say that these texts are 'more than myth': they are also profound stories in which we may hear Earth telling her story and voicing her indictments regarding our treatment of our environment.

The volumes in the *Earth Bible Commentary* series are the natural extension of *The Earth Bible* series published in 2000–2002. I wish to thank David Clines and Sheffield Phoenix Press for resurrecting this series—it has already made a significant contribution to biblical hermeneutics. I also wish to thank Joh Wurst for her editing, and The Charles Strong Trust for its ongoing support.

Since this volume is the first in the series, it also includes a general introduction to the series. While this introduction articulates the key principles and steps associated with recent ecological hermeneutics—such as those found in the SBL Symposium volume, *Exploring Ecological Hermeneutics*—subsequent writers in this series are free to adapt this approach as they feel is appropriate for a given text and/or context.

Although the wider context for this volume is the current environmental crisis, the immediate context of this volume is the literary context in which the two myth cycles in Genesis are identified. To highlight the significance and centrality of the key domains/characters in these myth cycles, I have used the thematic Hebrew terms *Erets* and *Adamah* where appropriate.

In this volume I read these myths as an Earth being seeking to identify with, and to hear the voice of, *Erets*, *Adamah*, and any members of the living communities associated with these key domains/characters in the cosmos; and to discern levels of meaning that are 'more than myth' that invite us to relate to our environment as a network of vibrant living presences. The title of this volume focuses on three key themes of these myths that highlight distinctive experiences of Earth that are relevant in the context of the current environmental crisis.

Norman Habel
2010

ABBREVIATIONS

BJRL	*Bulletin of the John Rylands University Library of Manchester*
JSOT	*Journal for the Study of the Old Testament*
JSOTSup	*Journal for the Study of the Old Testament*, Supplement Series
repr	reprint
SBL	Society of Biblical Literature
SCM	Student Christian Movement
WW	*Word and World*
WWSup	*Word and World* Supplement

Chapter 1

Introducing The Earth Bible Commentary Series

The five volumes of *The Earth Bible* (2000–2002) represent a landmark in the development of an ecological approach to reading and interpreting the biblical text. The Earth Bible team situated in Adelaide, South Australia, and led by Norman Habel, formulated a set of principles in consultation with ecologists and representatives of other disciplines. The opening chapter in each volume of this series examines a key issue that emerged in response to this approach.

The aims of the Earth Bible project:

- to acknowledge, before reading the biblical text, that as Western interpreters we are heirs of a long anthropocentric, patriarchal and androcentric approach to reading the text that has devalued Earth and that continues to influence the way we read the text;
- to declare, before reading the text, that we are members of a human community that has exploited, oppressed and endangered the existence of the Earth community;
- to become progressively more conscious that we are also members of the endangered Earth community in dialogue with ancient texts;
- to recognize Earth as a subject in the text with which we seek to relate empathetically rather than as a topic to be analysed rationally;
- to take up the cause of justice for Earth and to ascertain whether Earth and the Earth community are oppressed, silenced or liberated in the text;
- to develop techniques of reading the text to discern and retrieve alternative traditions where the voice of Earth and Earth community has been suppressed.

To guide writers in achieving these aims, a set of ecojustice principles were articulated (Habel 2000b). These principles were developed over a number of years in dialogue with ecologists such as Charles Birch (1990). The principles articulated below were refined in consultations and workshops concerned with ecology in general, and ecological concerns linked to theology and the Bible more specifically.

The principle of intrinsic worth
The universe, Earth and all its components have intrinsic worth/ value.

The principle of interconnectedness
Earth is a community of interconnected living things that are mutually dependent on each other for life and survival.

The principle of voice
Earth is a subject capable of raising its voice in celebration and against injustice.

The principle of purpose
The universe, Earth and all its components are part of a dynamic cosmic design within which each piece has a place in the overall goal of that design.

The principle of mutual custodianship
Earth is a balanced and diverse domain where responsible custodians can function as partners with, rather than rulers over, Earth to sustain its balance and a diverse Earth community.

The principle of resistance
Earth and its components not only suffer from human injustices but actively resist them in the struggle for justice.

The various writers in the series focused on one or more of the six principles enunciated in volume one of *The Earth Bible* series and explored the way in which those principles were either supported or suppressed in a given biblical text. The overall aim of the writers was to read the text 'from the perspective of Earth and/or the Earth community'.

Our approach in this new *Earth Bible Commentary* series attempts to move beyond a focus on ecological themes to a process of listening to, and identifying with, Earth as a presence or voice in the text. Our task is to take up the cause of Earth and the non-human members of the Earth community by sensing their presence in the text—whether their presence is suppressed, oppressed or celebrated. We seek to move beyond identifying ecological themes in creation theology to identifying with Earth in its ecojustice struggles.

After consideration of the various critiques of the Earth Bible principles, dialogue within the Earth Bible team and an analysis of so-called second level hermeneutical approaches—such as feminism and postcolonial hermeneutics—a more precise set of steps was developed for exploration as part of a Consultation for Ecological Hermeneutics at the annual meetings of the SBL (Society of Biblical Literature). These meetings were held in the USA between 2004 and 2008, again under the leadership of Norman

Habel. Since that date ecological hermeneutics has been included as a regular session of the SBL meetings.

This led to the reformulation of the principles enunciated in *The Earth Bible* as a hermeneutic of suspicion, identification and retrieval. The approach was developed through the papers and research of that consultation. Selected papers from that consultation were then published in a SBL symposium volume entitled *Exploring Ecological Hermeneutics* in 2008 (a summary of the fundamental hermeneutical steps outlined below are also found in the introduction to this volume; Habel 2008a).

In a subsequent volume, *An Inconvenient Text: Is a Green Reading of the Bible Possible?*, the assumptions and technique of ecological hermeneutics were developed further in relation to a series of key biblical texts where God is associated with nature (Habel 2009). A major feature in this study is the classification of biblical texts as 'green' or 'grey'. Green texts are those texts where nature, creation or the Earth community is affirmed, valued and recognized as having a role and a voice. Grey texts are those texts where nature, creation or the Earth community is devalued, oppressed, deprived of a voice or made subject to various forms of injustice at the hands of humans or God.

It is important to recognize that the identification of texts as green or grey is grounded in an ecological hermeneutic and is not to be confused with the identification of texts as green in *The Green Bible* (2008). This volume prints in green any text that relates to creation, nature or living beings without any apparent critical awareness of an ecological hermeneutics.

A revised ecological hermeneutic requires a radical re-orientation to the biblical text. The task before us is not an exploration of what a given text may say *about* creation, *about* nature, or *about* Earth. In this context, Earth is not a *topos* or theme for analysis. We are not focusing on ecology *and* creation, or ecology *and* theology (Habel 2000d). An ecological hermeneutic demands a radical change of posture both in relation to Earth as a subject in the text and also our relation to Earth as readers. Here the term 'Earth' refers to the total ecosystem, the web of life, the domains of nature with which we are familiar, of which we are an integral part and in which we face the future.

1. Context—The Environmental Crisis

No biblical interpreter reads the text in a vacuum. One or more living contexts are likely to influence both our conscious choice of a specific approach when reading the text and also our associated worldview, orientation or cosmology as contemporary readers. Two dimensions of our current context are explicit: our environmental crisis and our ecological orientation. The degree to which readers in this commentary series interact with either of these contexts will no doubt vary, depending on their particular text and context.

We read the text today in the midst of a global environmental crisis. The disastrous effects of climate change surround us as readers. If we dare to stand, for example, on the shore near Puri in Orissa and look out into the Bay of Bengal, we can see sand bars shining golden in the sun. The local fishermen may remind us that only a few years ago a village covered those sand bars. In the past 15 years the sea has encroached five kilometres and destroyed several such villages. Islands in the Pacific are waiting for the day when the seas will engulf them. For the villages on the shores of Orissa that day has come. The reader may then wonder about the words of Wisdom in Proverbs:

> God assigned the sea its limit, so that the waters might not transgress his command (Prov. 8.29).

Palaeoclimatologists may be able to demonstrate that our planet has undergone a range of climate cycles in its history. Climate change has been a feature of this planet's history from its beginnings (Jenson 2006: 201). The current change in climate, however, is a frightening fact and the current evidence indicates that the cause is not necessarily volcanic eruptions, variations in Earth's orbit around the sun or some meteorological phenomenon. The problem is the greedy way humans have exploited our fossil fuels and pumped greenhouse gases into the atmosphere at random.

Climate change has produced hot spots and intense weather experiences that differ radically from past weather patterns. In the state of Victoria in Australia, for example, the bushfires of Black Saturday in February 2009 are evidence of one such hot spot. On that Black Saturday, all the known patterns of a typical Australian bushfire were transcended.

Instead of plumes of swirling smoke and burning leaves flying into the sky, imagine a tornado with massive balls of fire leaping over an entire valley and landing on houses on the opposite hillside. The height and force of the typical bushfire has changed.

Instead of ferocious flames fanned by a hot North wind, imagine a hurricane Katrina, with temperatures of 110 degrees Fahrenheit, wind blasts of over 100 miles an hour and fierce fires—like open mouths, consuming all in their path. The heat and energy of the typical bushfire has changed. According to one analyst, the inferno generated enough 'energy to fuel 1500 atomic bombs the size of Hiroshima' (*Adelaide Advertiser*, Friday 22 May 2009).

It seems we are entering a new age: a 'Greenhouse Age' in which the ecosystems of Earth will necessarily have to adapt to the new gases in her lungs. Lovelock reminds us that the

> few things we do know about the response of the Earth to our presence are deeply disturbing. Even if we stopped immediately all seizing of Gaia's land

and water for food and fuel production and stopped poisoning the air, it would take Earth more than a thousand years to recover from the damage we have done (2006: 6).

As we read the biblical text we are surrounded by a range of serious environmental crises which are liable to impact on the way we interpret the text. We are reading in a climate-changing context that is threatening to affect the future of our planet.

2. Context—An Ecological Worldview

In his general audience address in January 2001, Pope John Paul II introduced the need for an *ecological conversion*. Catholic theologians such as Denis Edwards have promoted this concept as integral to the development of ecotheology (2006: 2-4). The context for this concept is the growing ecological crisis and our emerging awareness of its implications. The dilemma before us is the way we understand this laudable idea. In the words of Edwards,

> [c]ommitment to ecology has not yet taken its central place in Christian self-understanding. It is far from central in terms of its structure, personnel and the struggle of justice and to the side of women in their struggle for full equality, so the church itself is called to conversion to the side of suffering creation (2006: 3).

If this conversion means taking a stand at the side of suffering creation, joining the struggle for ecojustice and seeking to heal the wounds of our planet, the process is indeed worthy and vital. In this context, the question at hand is how ecology contributes to our worldview or cosmology, and how, in turn, this new ecological awareness influences our interpretation of biblical tradition.

Another way of addressing this challenge is to speak of 'greening' our world and our way of thinking. In the past, 'greening' has been viewed as a rather trite popular term for eccentrics in the ecological movement. The term 'green', however, has come of age and is now employed to identify the orientation of those seeking to integrate ecology with a range of fields of thought and action. To be 'green' is to empathize with nature.

We are faced, it seems, with a new view of the natural world, a new understanding of the universe, a new cosmology that has little in common with the biblical, the geocentric, or the heliocentric cosmologies of the past. We are becoming aware of an ecocosmology: a worldview where ecology conditions our thinking.

Many writers still view ecology as but one scientific discipline among many. In reality, ecology has now become an integral part of our social, political and personal worlds. And if we are to face the challenge of ecology in biblical studies we need to articulate what ecology really means as part of our emerging worldview. How might we describe the essence of ecology that informs this emerging worldview? One option is the formulation of Thomas Berry.

> In reality there is a single integral community of the Earth that includes all its component members whether human or other than human. In this community every being has its own role to fulfil, its own dignity, its inner spontaneity. Every being has its own voice. Every being declares itself to the entire universe. Every being enters into communion with other beings. This capacity for relatedness, for presence to other beings, for spontaneity in action, is a capacity possessed by every mode of being throughout the entire universe. So too every being has rights to be recognised and revered (1999: 4).

Writers like Lorraine Code speak of ecology as

> a study of habitats both physical and social where people endeavour to live well together; of ways of knowing that foster or thwart such living; and thus of the ethos and habitus enacted in the knowledge and actions, customs, social structures and creative-regulative principles by which people strive or fail to achieve this realizable end (2006: 25).

In our current cosmology or ecology informed view of life in the natural world—and more particularly of Earth—I would suggest we become conscious of the following understandings.

- Earth is a planet that originated in cosmic space and evolved into a living habitat that influences how we act and think; in this habitat humans are living expressions of the cosmos.
- Earth is a fragile web of interconnected and interdependent forces and domains of existence that not only interact and but create complex identities in diverse worlds; in this web humans are intelligent carbon creatures.
- Earth is a living community in which humans and all other organisms are kin who live and move and influence each other's destinies and perceptions of those destinies; in this community humans are conscious Earth beings.

Earth is a living planet. All of its components—from the mountains to the forests, from the oceans to the Antarctic—are part of this complex living entity called Earth. And human beings, along with all other living beings, are privileged to be an integral part of this living planet. Not only is Earth a unique living planet in our galaxy; Earth provides the habitat in which we live and nurtures all consciousness as we know it. We no longer dwell 'on Earth'; we live 'in Earth'. Earth is our habitat, our home, and our mentor. Earth is a complex world that influences how we live, move, and think about our being. In this world we are an expression of the cosmos; we are beings informed by the evolution of all galaxies and planets.

Earth is a fragile web of interconnectedness. As human beings we are not separate or disconnected from the various forces and domains of nature. We are totally dependent on the various ecosystems of Earth for survival; Earth's ecosystems have existed for millennia. The movement of oxygen in the atmosphere is necessary for us to breathe. The movement of moisture in the clouds and the seas is essential for us to enjoy a drink. The movement of worms in the soil is vital for us to receive our daily bread. Ultimately, we are carbon creatures totally interconnected with all other animate and inanimate carbon domains.

The reality that we are Earth is expressed well in the following statement:

> Matter is made from rock and soil. It, too, is pulled by the moon as the magma circulates through the planet heart and roots such molecules into biology. Earth pours through us, replacing each cell in the body every seven years. Ashes to ashes, dust to dust, we ingest, incorporate and excrete the earth, are made from earth. I am that. You are that! (Macy 1996: 501).

Earth is also a community of kin. Recent research in biology, genetics and evolutionary science has reminded us that we are kin with all other living things on Earth. As human beings we are related to all living things; some creatures are close relatives and others are distant kin. Some seem friendly and others fierce. But we are related to all—whether they are ants or elephants, sea horses or hidden organisms. Deep within, the genetic coding of humans is little different from that of most other animals. We belong to the same family, a community of kin.

Beyond the strictly biological and geological interdependency we experience, this habitat called Earth is composed of a complex world of presences that impinge upon us from birth to death, forming and transforming us as Earth beings, human beings and thinking beings. From towering mountains and threatening storms to delicate wings of butterflies and so-called weeds that invade our gardens, we are enveloped by environmental influences that mould our minds.

Berry (1999: 4) maintains that there is a capacity in all beings to enter into communion with other beings. Living beings are not only biologically related; they also possess an inner impulse to commune with other beings and to relate to the universe. The research of scholars such as Ursula Goodenough illustrates that numerous modes of communication, awareness and communion characterize living beings in Earth's diverse family (Goodenough 1998).

As we read the text we are now acutely conscious that we are Earth beings; that Earth is our habitat in the cosmos; that we part of a kinship called Earth community.

3. *Suspicion—Anthropocentric Bias*

A radical ecological approach to the text involves a basic hermeneutic of suspicion, identification and retrieval. This progression bears obvious similarities with several approaches of well-known feminist hermeneutics. The difference, of course, is that we are not reading from within the worldview of women, but first and foremost from within the orientation of an ecosystem called Earth. We are not identifying with women in the text on the basis of our experiences, but with non-human characters and habitats within the plot of the narrative. We are reading as Earth beings: members of the Earth community in solidarity with Earth.

First, we begin reading with the suspicion that the text is likely to be inherently anthropocentric and/or has traditionally been read from an anthropocentric perspective. At the outset, anthropocentric needs to be distinguished from two related terms: anthropogenic—a text originating from humans; anthropotopic—a text in which humans are a central *topos* or theme.

The anthropocentric bias that we are likely to find both in ourselves as readers and in the text we are reading has at least two faces. First, the assumption or condition we have inherited as human beings especially in the Western world: that we are beings of a totally different order than all other creatures in nature; in other words, in the hierarchy of things there is God, human beings, and the rest. Even where scholars have insisted that texts are theocentric rather than anthropocentric in character, the writer may ultimately be more concerned about God's relation to humanity or a group within humanity than about God's relation to Earth or the Earth community as a whole.

The Bible has long been understood as God's book for humans. And for those of us who have been reading biblical texts that way for years, this understanding has come to be self-evident. Should we not then, with a new ecological consciousness, legitimately suspect that the text and its interpreters have been understandably anthropocentric?

A second face of our anthropocentric bias is the assumption that nature is 'object', never subject. We have for so long viewed nature and all its parts—both animate and inanimate—as the object of many forms of human investigation, of which scientific analysis is but one. This process has not only reinforced a sense of human superiority over nature; it has also contributed to a sense of distance, separation and otherness. The rest of nature, especially the inanimate world, has been viewed as separate, other, and a force to be harnessed and subjected.

This phase of the hermeneutical process is related especially to the principle of intrinsic worth articulated in *The Earth Bible* (see Habel 2000b). When viewed through a traditional anthropocentric bias, other parts of nature are considered of less value. Often they are viewed merely as the stage, scenery or background for God's relationship with humanity. They are seldom regarded as valued subjects in their own right.

One of the reasons for this anthropocentric blind spot in our interpretive work as readers of an ancient text is that we are still influenced by traditional dualisms about reality. This view of reality has only developed since biblical days but because these dualisms are so much part of our Western view of reality, we may assume they are an inherent aspect of the biblical text. The key elements of the dualistic structure of Western thought are outlined by Plumwood (1993: 43). These include, among others, the following sets of contrasting pairs:

culture	/	nature
reason	/	nature
male	/	female
mind, spirit	/	body (nature)
reason	/	matter
reason	/	emotion (nature)
rationality	/	animality (nature)
human	/	nature (non-human)
civilized	/	primitive (nature)
production	/	reproduction (nature)
freedom	/	necessity (nature)
subject	/	object

To this listing, in the context of our project, I would add the following closely related pairs:

animate	/	inanimate
spiritual	/	material
heavenly	/	earthly
heaven	/	earth
sacred	/	profane

It is immediately apparent from these pairings that the realities associated with the human pole of the pairing are understood to be superior in some way to the nature pole of the pairing. These dualisms necessarily devalue Earth as inferior. Perhaps the most destructive form of this dualism developed as a result of the mechanistic approach of Descartes and his successors. According to Ponting, Cartesian dualism was

> reinforced by a mechanistic approach to natural phenomena, which can again be traced back to Descartes who wrote, 'I do not recognise any difference between the machines made by craftsmen and the various bodies that nature alone composes'...His mechanistic view of the world seemed to be vindicated by the spectacular success of Newton in the late seventeenth century in applying physical laws, such as that governing the force of gravity, to explain the workings of the universe (1991: 147).

Ecofeminists have also recognized a social and symbolic connection between the oppression of women and the domination of nature. When Earth has been viewed as female—Mother Earth or Mother Nature—Earth has often been abused and denied its rights. Eaton contends that as

> European societies developed, the combined influences of the rise of science, the dualisms of the Christian worldview, the philosophy of modernity and the industrialisation of the economy became the cultural forces that entrenched the feminising of nature…The influence of hierarchical dualisms, a core piece of patriarchal ideology and described by Habel in this volume, is central to feminist critiques (2000: 55).

We also read, therefore, with the suspicion that, in Western culture, the text has traditionally been interpreted from a dualistic perspective, regardless of the basic cosmology or sociology of the text. An ecological hermeneutic begins with the suspicion that text and interpreter may reflect an anthropocentric bias which is part of a wider Western dualistic orientation to the universe.

4. *Identification—Empathy with Earth*

The second element of a contemporary radical ecological hermeneutic is the task of empathy or identification.

In the light of my experience as an editor and writer in the Earth Bible project, it has become clear that the activity of identification now deserves to be highlighted as a distinct step in the hermeneutical process. As human beings we identify, often unconsciously, with the various human characters in the biblical story, whether that be an empathetic or antipathetic identification. We can identify with the experiences of these characters— even when we do not necessarily admire or would not seek to emulate the individuals.

Even before reading the narrative or poetry of the text, readers using this approach must—at least to some extent—come to terms with their deep ecological connections. Before we begin reading and seeking to identify with Earth in the text we need to face the prior ecological reality of our kinship with Earth: we are born of Earth, and we are living expressions of the ecosystem that has emerged on this planet. Our identities are influenced by the various environmental influences we experience in a given habitat. This step relates to the fundamental principle of interconnectedness explored in *The Earth Bible*.

Identification with Earth and members of the Earth community raises our consciousness to the injustices against Earth reflected in the text— and portrayed as consequences of both the actions of humans and God. Exegetes who pursue a radical ecological approach ultimately take up the cause of the natural world, seeking to expose the wrongs that Earth has suffered, largely in silence, and to discern, where possible, the way Earth has resisted these wrongs. Our aim is to read in solidarity with Earth. We are Earth beings reading in empathy with Earth.

Our approach is to move beyond a focus on ecological themes to a process of listening to, and identifying with, the Earth as a presence, character or voice in the text. Our task is to take up the cause of Earth and the non-human members of the Earth community by sensing their presence in the text—whether their presence is suppressed, oppressed or celebrated. We seek to move beyond identifying ecological themes in creation theology to identifying with Earth and the Earth community in their struggle for ecojustice.

The most obvious dimension of this step is to identify with non-human figures in the narrative, empathizing with their roles, characters and treatment, and discerning their voices. Another dimension of this process is to locate ourselves in the habitat of all the participants in the narrative, and discerning any forces, whether positive or negative, interacting with the characters in the text and determining their identities. These interactions may reveal how entities have been isolated, suppressed or devalued by the dominant figures and forces in their habitat.

The wisdom school's texts, such as Job and Proverbs, provide an interesting parallel to this approach of discerning both the character and habitat of every entity. In this school of thought, the essential character of any part of nature is its *derek* (way) and each entity in nature has its intended *maqom* (place or habitat) in the universe. An important task of the wise in this school was to discern the *derek* and *maqom* of each domain, entity or being in nature. That is precisely the challenge God presents Job in the speech from the whirlwind (Job 38–39). And in Job 28, even God seeks to discern both the 'way' and the 'place' of wisdom, searching everywhere on Earth beneath the heavens in the process (Habel 2003b).

In this step, when we read the text as Earth beings, we seek to identify with one or more of the non-human characters in the text and to locate ourselves in their respective habitats to ascertain what forces or factors we might legitimately claim these characters experience.

5. Retrieval—The Voice of Earth

The third facet of this radical ecological hermeneutic is that of retrieval. Retrieval is closely related to the prior steps of suspicion and identification.

As the interpreter exposes the various anthropocentric dimensions of the text—the ways in which the human agenda and biases are sustained either by the reader or the implied author—the text may reveal a number of surprises about the non-human characters in the story. Earth or members of the Earth community may be revealed as playing a key role or be highly valued in the text, but because of the Western interpretative tradition we have inherited, this dimension of the text has been ignored or suppressed.

Where we meet non-human figures communicating in some way—mourning, praising or singing—we have tended in the past to dismiss these expressions as poetic license or symbolic language. Our anthropocentric bias leads us to classifying these elements as mere anthropomorphisms.

Discerning Earth and members of the Earth community as subjects with voices is a key part of the retrieval process. In some contexts their voices are evident but have been traditionally ignored by exegetes. In other contexts their voices are not explicit, but nevertheless present and powerful though silent. These non-human subjects play roles in the text that are more than mere scenery or secondary images. Their voices need to be heard; their voices may not correspond to the languages and words we commonly associate with human voices.

To illustrate this point, we might turn to the prophets. In a number of passages in Jeremiah we are told the land is mourning (Jer. 4.28; 12.11). A close reading reveals that the text includes a double entendre that could be rendered 'dries up'. The physical act of 'drying up' is a way of expressing Earth mourning. The parallel to Earth 'drying up/mourning' in Jer. 4.18 is the sky becoming dark. Physical acts such as drying up, becoming dark, and quaking are ways in which parts of the Earth community communicate, in this case their grief. This form of communication even reaches Yhwh in Jer. 12.11.

Discerning this voice may even take the form of reconstructing the narrative—as a dimension of the interpretation process—in such a way as to hear Earth as the narrator of the story. In the process, Earth becomes an interpreter. Such a reconstruction is, of course, not the original text, but a reading as valid, I would argue, as the numerous efforts of biblical scholars over the centuries to reconstruct the history, literary sources, social world or theology behind a text.

The essence of this approach is expressed quite clearly by Hilary Marlow in an article on Amos. Marlow asks how

> can I have read the book of Amos so many times and not noticed the part the natural world plays within it? Why have I allowed my anthropocentric bias to muffle the voices of the rest of creation?

> The questions raised by the Earth Bible project include asking whether Earth is an active voice in the text or a passive lifeless entity, and if Earth is treated unjustly, and if so, to what extent that is acknowledged in the text. These concerns have promoted my re-examination of the text of Amos and a discovery that the natural world is an active participant in the Earth's story in this book (2008: 75).

The task before us is to re-read the text to discern where Earth or members of the Earth community may have suffered, resisted or been excluded by attitudes within the text or in the history of its interpretation.

Retrieval demands a strategy for reclaiming the sufferings and struggles of Earth, a task that involves regarding the wider Earth community as our kin. The aim is to read as Earth beings in tune with Earth, the very source of our being.

There is a strong possibility that biblical texts may be more sympathetic to the plight and potential of Earth than our previous interpretations have allowed, even if the ecological questions we are posing arise out of a contemporary Earth consciousness. We also need to consider the possibility that there are suppressed Earth traditions that resist the dominant patriarchal anthropocentric orientation of the text. By counter-reading the text it may be possible to identify alternative voices that challenge or subvert the normative voice of the dominant tradition. Whether these subtexts point to the continuing voice of ancient traditions still in touch with Earth, or whether these alterative perspectives arose as a mode of resisting the patriarchal orientation of monotheistic Yahwism, is a task for interpreters in this series to explore.

Especially significant in this context is the contribution of feminists and ecofeminists. Not only have they focused on identifying the patriarchal orientation and bias of both text and interpreter, they have also developed techniques of 'reading against the grain' and discerning traces of anti-patriarchal resistance in the text. Clues are sought within the text that point to traditions where the suppressed voices of women resisting a patriarchal society can be detected and the tradition itself may be retrieved. Ultimately, writes Schüssler Fiorenza,

> [r]ather than abandon the memory of our fore-sisters' sufferings, visions and hopes in our patriarchal biblical past, such a hermeneutics reclaims their sufferings, struggles, and victories through the subversive power of the 'remembered' past (1985: 133).

This technique of retrieval has been developed in a more 'revolutionary' way by feminists such as Pardes who discerns counter-traditions, subtexts that read against the grain of the dominant rhetoric of the main text. The patriarchy of the Bible is 'continuously challenged by antithetical trends' that need to be uncovered (Pardes 1992: 51). Pardes's goal is 'to reconstruct, in the light of surviving remains, antithetical undercurrents which call into question the monotheistic repression of femininity' (1992: 2).

Similarly, interpreters employing an ecological hermeneutic may pursue counter-readings that seek to retrieve elements of resistance, hidden undercurrents and suppressed voices that reflect the perspective of Earth or the Earth community and challenge the dominant anthropocentric voices of the biblical text. These suppressed elements provide the basis for reconstructing the voices of Earth and the domains of Earth that have been silenced by traditional readings.

6. *Contexts—Literary and Cultural*

Fundamental to any close reading of the text is a detailed analysis of the literary dimensions of the materials being examined. A priori is a consideration of the literary form of the text. Is it a hymn, a myth, a legend, an oracle or some other literary genre that is being employed to present the materials? How has the narrator incorporated this literary unit in the wider literary context? And in so doing, has a literary design been created that highlights the specific orientation of the narrator?

In the light of the preceding hermeneutics of suspicion, identification and retrieval, we may ask whether the narrator or compiler designs the material in such a way as to highlight the human characters rather than the non-human dimensions of the text. Or is there a subtle way in which the narrator has sympathized with Earth or members of the Earth community by using a particular genre that we, as anthropocentric and Western interpreters, have not discerned? Is the narrator conscious of being an Earth being as well as a human being?

Moreover, as we review the history of interpretation of a given biblical text we will discover numerous connections that have made between components in the text and the intertextual context. Past readings may have also contributed to a widely accepted understanding of the terminology, symbols and concepts of the text. A radical ecological reading dares to test these understandings, taking into account both the hermeneutics and the ecological context enunciated above.

Intertextual connections between a given text and related texts have played a significant role in biblical interpretation in recent years. A text is no longer viewed as a text in isolation, but connected with a wider context of passages where the same topic, terminology or symbol system is present. The interpreter can no longer ignore, for example, the possible connections between the *imago Dei* text in Gen. 1.26 and references to the image of God in Gen. 5.1 and 9.1-6. Do the latter passages provide evidence for a particular nuance of meaning in Gen. 1.26? Do they indicate the inclusion of a myth that might be designated the *Tselem* (image) myth?

Cultural connections are also important in seeking to discern the symbolic or metaphorical dimensions of the text. In an ancient Near Eastern world where the images of deities were common and where Aaron constructed an image for the people of Israel at Sinai, the particular connotation of the image of a deity in Gen. 1.26 cannot be ignored.

Nor can we ignore the widely accepted connection between the image of

God in Gen. 1.26-28 and the practice of certain ancient Near Eastern kings who erected images of themselves throughout their empires to proclaim their jurisdiction over a given domain. This connection has been cited to justify the royal imagery of the text and the ruling of humans a God's representatives.

A review of the traditional readings of the *imago Dei* in Gen. 1.26, for example, leads us to suspect that these intertextual and cultural connections have been read in the light of a dualistic understanding of reality. The image of God in humans has been widely understood as a non-physical dimension of human beings, such as reason, consciousness, or capacity to worship. And this dualistic anthropocentric mindset has influenced the interpretation of the nature and function of the *imago Dei* in the text of Gen. 1.26-28. We are led, therefore, through an intertextual 'green' reading to ask what the *imago Dei* might mean if we dare to identify not with the humans of the text, but with those domains over which humans are given dominion. Our aim is to read as Earth beings from within the habitat of Earth.

Various writers in this series may well identify connections with other contexts and approaches that are relevant in discerning the meaning of the text from the perspective of Earth and the Earth community. Crucial in the assessment of these connections is the ecological hermeneutic of suspicion identification and retrieval outlined above.

7. Application

This basic hermeneutic of suspicion, identification and retrieval will be employed by the writers in this series, not in a pedantic way, but in a manner that facilitates a genuine ecological interpretation of the text or book involved. Nor will interpreters necessarily follow a traditional pattern of examining all the textual and exegetical debates associated with a given text or textual unit. Writers are free to focus on those texts which uncover insights and issues that this approach highlights and to note the obvious anthropocentric biases of past interpreters that have blinded us to ecological or 'green' dimensions of the text.

It is also expected that each interpreter will re-examine the literary dimensions of the text to ascertain whether past examinations of the plot or structure of the unit under investigation have tended to be governed predominantly by an interest in the human subjects involved. Earth or members of the Earth community may well be characters in the narrative rather than mere scenery.

This hermeneutical approach needs to be distinguished from the reader-centred approach represented by Tim Meadowcroft in the new series published by Sheffield Phoenix Press. Meadowcroft, in his reading of Haggai, quite legitimately seeks to discern the relevance of a text for the reader in a given contemporary context by exploring how the intention of the text/author might speak to the modern reader. In connection with the current environmental crisis he writes that

> the church has an important role to play in calling people in this direction, not least because the call to rebuild the temple and the call for a sustainable approach to the environment are closely related concepts (2006: 240).

We are Earth beings, not merely human beings. As such we are invited to read from the perspective of Earth, and from within this habitat called Earth. This is the invitation extended to authors of *The Earth Bible Commentary* and to you as readers of this commentary series.

Chapter 2

Introducing Genesis 1–11

1. Basic Approach to Reading

a. Design

My ecological reading of Genesis 1–11 will first take into account the basic literary units that have traditionally been identified in these opening chapters of Genesis. Each chapter, therefore, will begin by examining the literary structure or design of the unit being considered. This investigation of the design, however, will take into account non-human characters or components as legitimate determining factors in the structuring of the narrative.

Where appropriate a typical structural analysis or design by a representative biblical scholar will be cited to illustrate the anthropocentric bias typical of such analyses in the past. My own structural analysis will recognize Earth, domains of Earth, and members of the Earth community as valid subjects in the design of the narrative.

As a result, the design of the narrative may highlight dimensions of the text that have been ignored or dismissed in the past but which demand special attention when reading the narrative from an ecological perspective.

In this context, I will not elaborate on the possible literary sources of the text, a task I undertook with my students more than forty years ago (Habel 1971). Nor will I pursue a form critical or tradition critical analysis. Rather, my concern will be on how the narrative design of the text reflects the way in which Earth, domains of Earth, or members of the Earth community are represented and given voice in the narrative.

b. Analysis

My analysis of plot, characters and meaning will flow from the structural design of the narrative in the preceding section. Textual units will be examined as coherent units of plot or thought. This analysis will take into account typical anthropocentric and dualistic readings of the text by past scholars that illustrate the limitations of past approaches, but will not engage in lengthy dialogue with the numerous interpreters of these famous chapters.

Integral to my reading of the text will be an orientation of empathy and concern for Earth as such, for domains of Earth such *Erets* or *Adamah*, and for members of the Earth community such as the snake. The task is to ascertain what role the characters play as subjects in the plot and in the meaning of the narrative—whether or not that role is made explicit by the narrator. By identifying with these non-human characters or domains in the narrative, we read the text with new eyes and can often discern dimensions that may otherwise be overlooked.

Careful consideration will be given to the nuances of meaning found in the use of key terms, word plays, rhetorical innuendoes, intertextual associations, mythic dimensions, and cultural imagery. Special attention will be paid to how the natural world is depicted and whether subjects from that world emerge as components that deserve special consideration in terms of the habitat reflected in the textual world. Attention will also be given to connections that have traditionally been made with symbols, concepts or language from the cultural contexts of the ancient Near Eastern world and their viability assessed in terms of an ecological hermeneutic.

At key points, we may move from the analysis of specific words, images or textual units to focus on the broader ecological patterns or issues that emerge. While a detailed knowledge of the biblical Hebrew and the ancient Near Eastern context is assumed, we will not necessarily debate the original form of each grammatical expression. The focus will be on the language of the narrative and the meaning expressed, implied or hidden in that language when reading from the perspective of Earth and employing an ecological hermeneutic of suspicion, identification and retrieval.

c. *Retrieval*

By identifying and empathising with Earth or members of the Earth community, our analysis will usually retrieve dimensions of the text that have been ignored or dismissed. By locating as readers within the various habitats found in the text, we may also become conscious of factors and forces that inform the meaning of the passage. In the retrieval section, however, we go a step further and listen to the voice of the leading non-human character or characters in the narrative context.

The reconstruction of this voice, we would argue, is as legitimate as the efforts of scholars in the past who sought to reconstruct the social, historical or cultural world of the narrator/author from clues embedded in the text. Here we use textual clues to allow the key character to relate the story in the first person from a non-human perspective but conscious of the human audience. We may also read against the grain to discern the suppressed voices of oppressed non-human characters in the habitat they experience within the text.

As the key character relates the narrative from this new perspective, we gain a richer appreciation of the values once associated with nature that may have been lost and the many injustices that Earth and members of the natural world have experienced at the hands of humans and God in these narratives. The voice of this character may become a cry for justice that needs to be heard.

2. *Framework and Components of Genesis 1–11*

a. *The World of Myth*

Before outlining the structure and framework of Genesis 1–11, we need to recognize the importance of the literary forms or genres encompassed in this literary unit. The first and most significant genre is myth—especially origin myths and catastrophe myths. As part of their heritage, indigenous and ancient peoples throughout the world have origin myths; origin myths are a traditional way of making sense of the beginnings of the cosmos.

My research in this field has led me to identify three basic characteristics of origin myths (Habel 1993: 45). Origin myths assume a primordial world that precedes and leads to the known world of the people telling the myth. Time and space in the primordial world are of a different order to that evident in the known world. The boundaries of the primordial cosmos do not correspond to those of the known physical world. The timeless darkness of the watery deep in Gen. 1.2, for example, does not correspond to our physical world.

An origin myth regularly announces or assumes a vital absence of something in the primordial world. The events described in the myth bring this absent thing into being and illuminate it in a variety of ways. This filling of an absence may then result in a series of events that lead to domains of the cosmos or the community known to those telling the myth. The absence of someone or something to care for the *Adamah* in Gen. 2.5 is a typical example of such an absence in origin myths.

Also typical of an origin myth is that the recognized laws of nature and relationships do not necessarily apply in the primordial. It is quite normal, for example, for a snake to walk or talk in the primordial, even if that seems strange in the world we experience.

My experience with Indigenous Australians has led me to appreciate that origin myths are not naive explanations of reality, but powerful expressions of the interconnection between humans, Earth, and the Earth community. Typical of Indigenous Australian myths is the Dreaming, a primordial power from the distant past that persists in the present. Every human being has a personal dreaming, a spiritual force connected with

- a part of creation or creature such as a kangaroo;
- a specific sacred site on the landscape;
- the land/country where the dreaming is located;
- the story/myth told about the origin of that dreaming.

In the myth, the story may, for example, revolve around the kangaroo man: a primordial being who can turn from a kangaroo into a human and vice verse because the two forms have the same Dreaming spirit. This example illustrates how people who live with myths as part of their real world of meaning may have a genuine affinity and connection with nature that is physical, social and spiritual. Myths often reflect a deep bond with nature.

In addition to origin myths *per se* we need to consider myths that have been designated 'catastrophe myths'. These myths are also, in general, located in the primordial or early post-primordial world. It is typical of a catastrophe myth that there is a crisis in creation or the primordial world that forces the gods to intervene, frequently in anger. The crisis is followed by the catastrophe itself. The outcome of the catastrophe is usually some change in the cosmos or society. A catastrophe myth may therefore also be a type of origin myth describing how an entity or condition originated in the post-catastrophe world.

David Clines argues that the reasons ancient catastrophe myths—such as the flood—take place are (i) the unfathomable will of the gods, (ii) some non-moral fault that has angered the gods and (iii) a moral sin on the part of humankind (1998: 509). In the famous *Gilgamesh* epic, no ethical reason is given for sending the flood. Punishment for human sin is not the rationale.

When we turn to the myths of Genesis 1–11, we may ask whether the narrator has a sense of cosmological distance from the myths being remembered, or whether these myths are a meaningful part of the narrator's life experience. Either way, if we dare to return to the living world of the myths in Genesis 1–11 and identify with the natural domains of the myth, we may capture again some of the live spiritual dimensions of the original myth.

b. *The Myths of Genesis 1–11*
I believe there are two major myth cycles incorporated in Genesis 1–11: the *Erets* myth and the *Adamah* myth. The *Erets* myth commences in Gen. 1.2: 'And *Erets* was…'. The primordial state of *Erets* is described; primordial events surrounding her appearance are announced; her emergence from the deep is celebrated; her role as a partner in creation is affirmed; her commission to provide sustenance for living creatures is announced.

The *Erets* myth reappears in the flood narrative. The crisis in creation is that all *basar* (flesh) has become corrupt and is no longer true to its inner nature. Elohim therefore decides to 'corrupt/destroy' *Erets* and in the process returns the natural world of *Erets* to the primordial state that existed in the beginning. After the flood *Erets* once again appears. A rainbow originates and Elohim establishes a covenant with *Erets* to secure a post-catastrophe future. The components of this catastrophe myth are examined in detail in the relevant chapters of this volume. My reconstruction of the *Erets* myth is in the appendix.

The second myth cycle in these chapters is the *Adamah* myth. In Gen. 2.5-7 there is no one to care for *Adamah*, so Yhwh takes some soil from *Adamah* and forms *adam*. Yhwh then causes trees to grow to create the forest of Eden. After the enlightenment of the primal pair of humans, *Adamah* is cursed by Yhwh. Outside Eden humans are still responsible for *Adamah* from which they were taken.

The *Adamah* myth also reappears in the flood narrative. The crisis here is the sinfulness of all *adam*. Yhwh decides to 'blot out' *adam* from the face of *Adamah* (Gen. 6.7). After the flood, Yhwh removes the curse from *Adamah* and stabilizes the seasons for *Adamah*. The components of this myth are examined in detail in the relevant chapters of this volume. My reconstruction of the *Adamah* myth is in the appendix.

There are also components of other myths interspersed within the narratives of Genesis 1–11. Perhaps the most notable is what I have designated the '*Tselem*' or 'image' myth. The *Tselem* myth (Gen. 1.26-28) interrupts the *Erets* myth. In the *Tselem* myth humans are made to look like God (or the gods); they are to bear the *tselem* of God and to rule over all creatures. All humans who descend from Adam bear the *tselem* of Adam and therefore the *tselem* of God. After the flood, God confirms the status of humans as bearers of God's *tselem* (Gen. 9.1-7). Killing a human is equivalent to smashing a *tselem* of God.

The origin myth fragment in Gen. 6.1-4, where 'sons of God' have intercourse with the daughters of *adam*, is another origin myth that helps to explain the existence of giants such as Goliath; this myth, however, seems to be an independent fragment that is not directly connected with any of the three origin myths cited above.

The tower of Babel narrative (Gen. 11.1-9) has been classified as both a myth and a legend. Either way, this section explains the origin of languages and culture on Earth.

c. *The Framework*
The three myths identified above, namely, the *Erets*, *Adamah* and *Tselem* myths, are narrated within a framework of *toledoth* and supplemented by a handful of transitional legends. The term *toledoth* is regularly translated 'generations' or 'family history' and normally refers to the genealogies of biblical ancestors.

In this literary unit (Gen. 1–11) there are a series of such *toledoth* covering genealogies and family histories from Adam to Terah. The narrator also applies this designation to the origins of *shamayim* and *Erets* (Gen. 2.4b). Thus, the various myths and legends are framed as if they are part of human history. Understandably, therefore, the narrative of Genesis 1–11 has traditionally been read from an anthropocentric perspective. Our task is to free these myths from their anthropocentric literary framework, and discern their intention as origin or catastrophe myths that informed Israel's latent understanding of the primordial and the world that emerged from the primordial.

The narrative framework also functions to facilitate a transition from the primordial world of myth to the known historical world of Abram and the land of Canaan where he is destined to sojourn. To achieve this, the narrator incorporates several legends about Canaan. These include the curse of Canaan; the names of peoples associated with Canaan; a postscript which recalls how Terah planned to go to Canaan but never actually arrived.

A further legend, which interrupts the extended *toledoth* that conclude the narrative framework, is that of the tower of Babel. This myth seeks to explain the origins of cultures—as distinct from the domains of the cosmos. This myth, however, is in tension with the closing legends associated with the *toledoth* of Canaan.

d. *Structural Outline*

The body of this volume provides my detailed analysis of the myths, legends, and framework summarized here. This structural outline provides a guide for readers.

Origin Myth
Erets myth—Gen. 1.1–2.3
Tselem myth—Gen. 1.26-28
       Framing: *toledoth* of *shamayim* and *Erets*—Gen. 2.4a
Origin Myth
    Adamah myth—Gen. 2.4b–3.24
    Adamah myth—Gen. 4.1-16
       Framing: *toledoth* of Cain—Gen. 4.17-26
       Framing: *toledoth* of Adam—Gen. 4.26–5.32
Origin Myths
    Tselem myth—Gen. 5.1-2
    Shamayim myth—Gen. 6.1-4
Catastrophe Myths
    Rationale: *Adamah* myth—Gen. 6.5-8
       Framing: *toledoth* of Noah—Gen. 6.9-10
    Rationale: *Erets* myth—Gen. 6.11-13
    Accounts (combined): *Adamah* myth & *Erets* myth—Gen. 6.14–8.19

Aftermath: *Adamah* myth—Gen. 8.20-22
    Tselem myth—Gen. 9.1-7
    Erets myth—Gen. 9.7-18
Culture Legend
  Curse of Canaan—Gen. 9.20-27
    Framing: *toledoth* of Noah's sons—Gen. 9.28–10.32
Culture Myth
  Babel Myth—Gen. 11.1-9
    Framing: *toledoth* of Shem—Gen. 11.10-26
    Framing: *toledoth* of Terah—Gen. 11.20-30
Culture Legend
  Families of Canaan—Gen. 10.15-20
  Journey to Canaan—11.31-32

Chapter 3

GENESIS 1.1–2.4A:
THE ORIGIN MYTH OF *ERETS* AND *SHAMAYIM*

1. *Design*

Understandably, many scholars have discerned the design of Gen. 1.1–2.4a
in terms of the seven days associated with this narrative. One or more
events are associated with each day; events are viewed as happening in
a logical sequence. Significantly, the climax in this sequence is believed
to be the creation of humans on the sixth day, a perception that may well
reflect the anthropocentric orientation of past interpreters as much as any
intrinsic structure in the narrative.

In his well-known work, *The Genesis Accounts of Creation* (1964),
Westermann recognized that there may be at least two structures within
the Genesis 1 account: first, a monotonous rhythm is characteristic of P
(1964: 7); second, colour and diversity of presentation is embedded within
the P narrative (1964: 12). He concedes that these two structures have
been fused to such an extent through the ongoing tradition that very few
cues are left to differentiate the two.

Even more significant, however, is Westermann's recognition that Gen.
1.26-28 is a 'rupture within the framework' of the narrative. He notes that
the

> P structure slips noticeably into the background. It is not recorded as a
> command and the fulfillment of this command, but as a resolution on God's
> part, and the fulfillment of this resolution. This serves to underline the
> uniqueness of man's [sic] creation. The creation of man [sic] is something far
> different from the creation of the rest of the world. One could say that this
> ruptures the framework of the course of creation (1964: 21).

One of the popular ways to view the design of Genesis 1 is to focus on the
creative acts of God and order them, as Middleton (2005: 278) has done,
into two symmetrical triads.

Preparation (Genesis 1.1–2.3)
(formless and empty)

Panel 1   Panel 2
(forming static regions)   *(filling with mobile occupants)*
Day One (Genesis 1.3-5)   Day Two (Genesis 1.14-19)
(1) light/darkness   (5) luminaries
Day Two (Genesis 1.6-8)   Day Five (Genesis 1.20-23)
(2) water/firmament/water   (6) fish and birds
Day Three (Genesis 1.9-13)   Day Six (Genesis 1.24-31)
(3) water/dry ground   (7) land animals
(4) vegetation   (8) humans

Day Seven (Genesis 2.1-3)
(the heavens, the earth and all their host)

When we approach the design of the passage from the perspective of the chief characters/domains and the primary events or actions in the narrative plot, alternative structural designs may emerge. The following design reflects an awareness of these characters and the way in which Gen. 1.26-28 represents a rupture in the basic framework of the narrative.

The Creation Narrative
Narrative Title (Genesis 1.1)
(God created sky and Earth)
Narrative Setting (Genesis 1.2)
Introducing the Primal Characters
Earth, waters and wind (of God)

Scene One (Genesis 1.3-5)   Scene Five (Genesis 1.14-19)
Light created by God and   *Lights* created by God in sky to
separated from darkness   give light for Earth and seasons
Scene Two (Genesis 1.6-8)   Scene Six (Genesis 1.20-22)
Waters separated by God   *Water* creatures emerge and
and *sky* made   *sky* creatures created
Scene Three (Genesis 1.9-10)   Scene Seven (Genesis 1.23-25)
Earth revealed from   *Earth* creatures emerge
beneath the waters   from Earth

Scene Eight (Genesis 1.26-28)
Humans created by God
to rule/subdue Earth

Scene Four (Genesis 1.11-13)   Scene Nine (Genesis 1.29-31)
Vegetation is brought   *Vegetation* given as food
forth by Earth   for all living creatures

Narrative Coda (Genesis 2.1-3)
God rests and blesses
the seventh day
Narrative Notation (Genesis 2.4a)
The family tree of sky and Earth

This design reflects an ordered narrative structure. In the interpretation that follows, we will follow the sequence of scenes in the narrative, recognizing that Gen. 1.26-28 is a deviation or rupture of the basic narrative pattern. The basic narrative pattern is typical of origin stories or primal myths found in the ancient Near East and numerous Indigenous cultures. These narratives regularly commence by outlining the dimensions of the primordial presence and primordial absence in the world according to the traditions of that culture. The various scenes of the narrative progressively describe how the primal world—especially its absence—is transformed into the present world or some domain of that world.

What distinguishes the Genesis 1 account from most other origin stories is the symmetrical pattern of the scenes. This symmetry may suggest artistic and poetic skill on the part of the narrator who retells this creation myth in a particular cultural context. This symmetry does not, however, justify classifying this narrative as a liturgy, as Brueggemann and others have done (1982: 33). The explicit repetition of lines and themes is as much part of primal narratives and storytelling as it is of liturgy.

If we identify with Earth as the first character introduced in this narrative, the progression of scenes reflects the stages in which Earth is revealed, made replete with all forms of life, and finally blessed by God. In this narrative sequence the 'goodness' of Earth and its living components are celebrated by God. Earth is, moreover, a partner with God in the creation of vegetation and other life forms.

Given this underlying basic narrative sequence, the creation of humans in vv. 26-28 is not only a rupture, as Westermann maintains, but also a violation of the role of the central character of the story. Earth is no longer a partner; Earth is an object of subjugation. Living creatures are no longer the celebrated progeny of Earth, but creatures to be dominated by humans. The full force of this conflict between the basic narrative and the scene where humans are created will be evident in the analysis which follows.

In spite of this obvious 'rupture' in the narrative of Earth, most interpreters argue that the creation and the creation event are to be viewed from the perspective of human beings. The alternative orientation of Earth, the main character in the account, is ignored. In the movement of the creation story outlined by Bernhard Anderson, for example, the climax of the story is human fertility and dominion over Earth. Humanity, claims Anderson, belongs to the 'sphere of God's cosmic administration' (1994: 50-52).

If we take a further step in analysing this design by recognizing that the text is a traditional origin myth, we can discern an even clearer focus on Earth (*Erets*) as the primary character and focus. If we also recognize the validity of the research of Ellen van Wolde that *bara* does not mean create but 'separate' (2009), we can refine the design of this text as a traditional myth of 'separation' and 'emanation/emergence'. After the domains of the primordial cosmos have been separated, new entities emanate from these domains as in other ancient origin myths. We also recognize that the rupture in the narrative sequence is caused by the intrusion of another myth, the *Tselem* myth, which has a radically different orientation.

The *Erets* Myth
A Myth of Separation and Emanation

Preamble (Genesis 1.1)
When Elohim separated *Erets* from *shamayim*
Setting: Primordial World (Genesis 1.2)
The primordial mythic cosmos;
Erets in waters of the deep & darkness below
wind of Elohim above

Scene One (Genesis 1.3-5): Separation	Scene Five (Genesis 1.14-19): Emanation
Light separated from	Lights set in *shamayim*; light
the primal darkness	emanates for *Erets* and seasons
Scene Two (Genesis 1.6-8): Separation	Scene Six (Genesis 1.20-22): Emanation
Primal waters separated	Water creatures emanate from waters
Waters above fixed by a *shamayim*	and birds fly in the *shamayim*
Scene Three (Genesis 1.9-10): Separation	Scene Seven (Genesis 1.23-25): Emanation
Waters separated before	land creatures emanate
Erets emerges from the waters	from *Erets*

Scene Eight (Genesis 1.26-28)
The *Tselem* myth: Separation & Domination
humans made with tselem of Elohim
& separated to rule/subdue *Erets*

Scene Four (Genesis 1.11-13): Emanation	Scene Nine (Genesis 1.29-31): Emanation
Vegetation emanates	Vegetation emanating from *Erets*
from *Erets*	is food for all living creatures

Scene Ten (Genesis 2.1-3): Separation
Elohim rests and separates
the seventh day as holy
Framing Coda (Genesis 2.4a)
The *toledoth* of *shamayim* and *Erets*

Given the centrality of *Erets* in this myth, the task of identifying with *Erets* and any of the related domains or emanations in this myth is perhaps made easier. In any case, as we proceed with a detailed analysis, we keep in mind that we are Earth beings seeking to connect with Earth and related characters; this makes this myth an important part of our heritage, even if we are living in a so-called enlightened world where evolution and ecology govern our cosmology.

2. *Analysis*

a. *Preamble*
The opening verse is probably a kind of ancient title or preamble summarizing the major thrust of the plot in this *Erets* myth, namely, God ordering and populating the physical universe consisting of *shamayim* and *Erets*. It is significant that our suspicion of dualistic thinking among traditional interpreters of Genesis 1 is confirmed in the traditional translation of the very first verse of the Bible. That the term *shamayim* does not mean 'heavens' is evident form the divine action of day two where God constructs the *shamayim* as a firmament or ceiling overhead. The Hebrew term '*shamayim*' means sky not heaven. There is no suggestion here of a dualistic universe consisting of a particular domain for God and celestial beings. Nowhere in Genesis 1 is heaven created as God's abode; rather, *Erets* and *shamayim* are the physical universe.

Genesis 1.1 has also been rendered as a subordinate clause: 'when God began creating sky and Earth'. Such a rendering, however, does not alter the substance of the verse, but simply points the reader immediately forward to the primordial state in Gen. 1.2. The opening line highlights what will happen to *Erets* and *shamayim* in the narrative that follows.

If the verb *bara* is rendered 'create'—as has traditionally been the case— all the events that follow will be viewed as God creating various domains of the world in one way or another.

If, however, we recognize with Ellen van Wolde that the Hebrew verb means 'separate', this myth is not about God 'creating' everything, but about stages of separating, ordering and activating domains of the cosmos.

> Thus, based on the internal and external linguistic and textual evidence and on a controlled argumentation, it is highly plausible and very likely that the type of action expressed by the verb *bara'* in Genesis 1 does not mean 'to create' but that it can be rendered by 'to separate', designating an action of a very concrete, special and physical character (2009: 20).

Following van Wolde's recommendation, therefore, we would render this opening preamble as 'In the beginning in which/when God separated *shamayim* and *Erets*'. This translation makes it clear that the events which follow are a description of how this 'separation' takes place and what ensues from this separation. The focus of the process which follows rests on *Erets* whose separation is not only climactic, but is also associated with a related birth metaphor of special significance.

b. *Setting (Genesis 1.2): Primordial World*
Typical of primordial or origin myths around the world, the setting outlines the dimensions of the primordial presence and absence. The reader

anticipates how these dimensions will be transformed in the process that follows. In the Genesis 1 narrative, the setting introduces the listener to three forces or domains which describe the primordial cosmos:

> *Erets*—described as *tohu wabohu* in the waters;
> waters—described as the deep *(tehom)* in darkness;
> wind—described as the *ruach* of Elohim hovering.

As a reader, I could potentially identify with any one of these domains introduced in the setting. The wind *(ruach)* of Elohim, as distinct from the voice of Elohim, plays no further role in the plot. The waters are an important domain that needs to be separated at key points in the plot. The first domain introduced, *Erets*, is a central figure and one with whom we may readily identify when we use an ecological hermeneutic.

What are these domains and how are they related in this opening verse? What is the habitat of *Erets* in the beginning? Later *Erets* is revealed to be the land mass on which fauna and flora can flourish. The primordial absence in the case of *Erets* is described as *tohu wabohu*. While there is considerable discussion about the specific meaning of this idiom, the textual evidence suggests an absence of form and fertility. Clearly, *Erets* exists, but as yet has not assumed its final shape or function and has not yet been filled with life forms. This transformation takes place in the course of the narrative. There are no specific indications within the setting itself that the idiom *tohu wabohu* means chaos in this text (cf. Tsumura 2005: ch. 1).

The term *tehom* (deep)—especially since the interpretation of Hermann Gunkel in the nineteenth century (1997; 2006)—has frequently been connected with *Tiamat*, the chaos waters deity found in the Babylonian *Enuma Elish* myth. The research of recent interpreters such as Tsumura (2005: ch. 2) has demonstrated that, whatever the origin of the term *tehom*, an association with chaos—and Tiamat in particular—should no longer be made in this context. The setting is a pre-creation scene in which the primal waters that extend into the deeps of the primal cosmos are simply present in anticipation of the transformations that ensue in the separation/creation process.

My findings are consistent with those of van Wolde.

> This is the primeval situation: no 'nothing', nor a chaos that needs sorting out, but a situation of 'before' or 'not yet' in view of what is coming. Even God is not yet the Creator, but an indefinable spirit of God moving on the face of the waters. These are the main characters of the story to come (1998: 25).

The wind *(ruach)* of God is an integral part of the primordial world; Hiebert suggests *ruach* is the atmosphere of the primal universe (2008: 10). This presence of God is not a raging storm but a breeze blowing across the 'face' of the waters. The use of the verb *rachaph* in Deut. 32.11, describing an eagle mother hovering over her young before teaching them to fly, suggests an image of parental nurture rather than primal disturbance. As Schottroff says, the 'brooding mother bird with fluttering wings is God's quickening breath, his invigorating and supportive spirit' (1993: 25).

If I now locate myself within the primordial habitat of *Erets* and identify with her as a character in this primal scene, I discover a number of forces around me. I am enveloped in waters called the deep. There is no indication that these waters are forces of chaos around me. I am also enveloped by darkness and hence not visible. I am also conscious that there is an atmosphere or wind: God is hovering above the waters where I am residing.

The imagery of this habitat or scene suggests an embryonic figure without the form and fertility later associated with that land mass called *Erets*. The scenario suggests a primal womb embracing the unborn *Erets*. It is a scene of anticipation rather than agitation, of calm rather than chaos, of the primal world before separation. God is present as a hovering wind—a presence more like a midwife or a parent than a raging storm; God is the potential atmosphere that will provide life-giving breath when *Erets* is born.

c. *Scene One (Genesis 1.3-5): Light Separated from Darkness*
The opening scene begins with a creative impulse from God expressed as Elohim speaking, using the idiom 'Let there be'. The creative power of the divine word is a tradition known from the Psalms (Ps. 33.6). Interpreters discern a range of theological implications in this divine mode of action. Within the narrative plot, however, God's word functions as the catalyst that initiates a diversity of actions in the various scenes of the narrative. God is not some distant divine being speaking from heaven, but is present at the scene.

When God speaks, the first action is the immediate advent of light. Elohim says 'Let there be light' and light appears. Light, which von Rad called 'the first-born of creation' (1961: 49), is not described in any way. This phenomenon is apparently self-evident to the narrator. Light is not equivalent to cosmic energy or some other scientific phenomenon; this account is a simple myth about the origin of a phenomenon we see every day. With the advent of light, the first divine act of separation is recorded: God separates light from darkness and consequently day from night.

What is the implied nature and function of light in the narrative? First, from the perspective of *Erets* in the primordial setting, the darkness that enveloped the waters where *Erets* was waiting to appear no longer dominates the scene. When she appears, *Erets* can now be seen. Light also enables *Erets*, waiting in the dark waters, to be seen before her birth.

d. *Scene Two (Genesis 1.6-8): Waters Separated and Sky Made*
In scene two the creative impulse of Elohim's word summons a *raqia* into existence. It is clear from the function of the *raqia* in the narrative that

this domain serves to separate the primal waters and hold some of them in a realm above. The *raqia* seems to be some kind of ceiling or dome that holds back the separated cosmic waters now located above. The idiom 'he who stretches out the heavens', found elsewhere in the Hebrew Scriptures, reflects a different tradition which views the skies as a tent stretched out for the appearing of Yhwh (Habel 1972). Unlike the appearance of light in scene one, the dome is explicitly 'made' by God, suggesting some kind of physical structure. The *raqia* is expressly named *shamayim*, and is the upper half of the physical universe announced in the preamble to the myth.

How is this scene related to the anticipated appearance of *Erets*—whose hidden presence in announced in the setting of the narrative in Gen. 1.2? From the perspective of *Erets*, this separation of the waters is not a conquest of the waters of chaos to form the two domains of *shamayim* and *Erets*. Rather, the formation of a solid realm above prepares the way for the appearance of *Erets*, a solid realm below. First, *Erets* emerges from the waters below and second, there is space beneath the *shamayim* into which the emerging *Erets* can move and be seen. Scene two sets the stage for the birth of *Erets* in scene three.

1. *The Birth Metaphor*. The implication of this reading that a womb/birth metaphor lies behind the imagery for the setting and appearance of *Erets* on day three may seem surprising, given the tendency of many interpreters to view *tehom* and the waters as evidence of primal chaos. That *Erets* has been viewed as a mother in some biblical passages is well known (Ps. 139.13-15). Job cries out, 'Naked I came from my mother's womb and naked I shall return there' (Job 1.21).

A primal birth image is explicit in passages such as Job 38.8 where sea comes forth from a primal womb to be clothed and contained by God. Immediately relevant is the imagery of Ps. 90.2 where the psalmist asserts that El, the creator God, was present before the mountains were born (*yld*) and before *Erets* and the inhabited world came to birth and was brought forth in labour (*chwl*). This passage quite explicitly speaks of the origins of *Erets* at the hands of the maker/midwife in terms of a birthing process—a tradition that I suggest is also reflected in Genesis 1 (cf. Anderson 1972: 650).

e. *Scene Three (Genesis 1.9-10): Waters Separated and Erets Born/Revealed*
Scene three is the first climax in this *Erets* myth. Waiting in the waters of the primal womb while light and space are formed, *Erets* is ready to make an appearance. It is a birth: first there is the parting of the waters and then the hidden form appears; separation precedes the appearance of *Erets*. This dual action is set in motion by Elohim.

Especially significant is the expression 'let dry land appear'. When the waters are separated and pulled back into their own domains, the revealed form of the *Erets* is described as *yabbasah*: a 'dry domain'. What once was enveloped in water is now visible dry land ready for life to inhabit. God then names this newborn domain *Erets*, 'Earth'—just as a human parent names a newborn human child.

The verb *raah* is usually rendered 'appear', though it could be translated 'be revealed'. The Niphal form of this verb used here is used elsewhere when God or an angel of God is revealed or 'appears'. In Gen. 18.1, 'Yhwh appeared to Abraham' (cf. Gen. 12.7; 35.1). The language of God's theophanic appearance to humans is here, in Gen. 1.9-10, associated with the appearance of *Erets*, highlighting the climactic significance of the event. The appearance of *Erets* might well be called a 'geophany' (cf. a theophany; see Habel 2000a: 34ff.).

This gives *Erets* a unique character, distinct from all other components of the cosmos. Only *Erets* is revealed from below, born out of the waters; *Erets* is a hidden mystery made manifest, a sacred domain in the cosmos.

When the light was separated from the darkness, Elohim—the character behind the breath and the voice—responds. Elohim not only speaks but also 'sees' in a distinctive way, responding personally to what appears and 'is seen'. Elohim does not pronounce light and Earth 'good', imprinting them with integrity from a position of authority. Rather, they 'are good' and God experiences them as such; Elohim 'sees' they are naturally good. The integrity of *Erets* is a given, discovered by God in the creation process.

The 'good' that Elohim sees in '*Erets* is not 'good' in some dualistic or moral sense. 'Good' is Elohim's response to what is seen, experienced in the moment of its appearance. A similar idiom is used to describe the response of Moses' mother when he is born. When she first bonds with the child 'she sees he is good' (Ex. 2.1). Elohim beholds Earth emerge from the waters below and 'sees Earth is good'. Elohim is delighted with the child who appears!

Appealing as it may be, there is no evidence in the text to suggest that *Erets* is an oppressed character within chaos waters who needs to be liberated (Deane-Drummond 1996: 17). The act of God separating the waters of the Reed Sea to expose the 'dry land' may have been a stage in the liberation of Israel, but the appearance of the dry land on the third day of the *Erets* myth is not a rescue operation; it is the revelation of a hidden reality, a birth, a separation from the waters below. Elohim, the god in Genesis 1, is not necessarily a prototype of Yhwh the Liberator in other passages of Scripture. The *Erets* story of Genesis 1 stands as an ancient origin myth in its own right.

If we recognize the validity of the birth metaphor, the progression from Gen. 1.2-10 becomes clear. A form, like an embryo, is located in the waters of the deep. These waters suggest a placid womb rather than a raging sea. Light and space are created so this form can be revealed. At the 'birth' moment, the waters separate/burst and—at the invitation of Elohim—the form appears/emerges out of the waters as a newborn child. God names this form 'Erets', looks at her and responds with delight.

f. Scene Four (Genesis 1.11-13): Erets Produces Vegetation

Elohim now speaks to the 'newborn' *Erets* and summons her to come alive, replete with all the vegetation typical of land; *Erets* comes to life by generating a range of plants complete with seeds that will enable regeneration. The immediate source of this plant life is not strictly the command of Elohim, but *Erets*—*Erets* is a partner with Elohim in the creation process, a co-creator. When the word of Elohim activates *Erets*, the potential life forces within *Erets* are activated and fauna and flora of all kinds emanate. The revealed *Erets* is the dormant source of all living creatures, except humans. Elohim observes what has appeared and declares it good; Earth's vegetation delights Elohim.

Identifying with *Erets* as a character in scenes three and four, I am a beautiful child in whom Elohim delights. I emerge when the primal womb parts. Fertility lies within me; I come alive and green, with the capacity to bring forth all kinds of vegetation.

g. Scene Five (Genesis 1.14-19): Lighting Erets

In scene five, Elohim fixes a range of lights in the *raqia* called *shamayim*. Significantly, these lights are not intended to adorn or illuminate the sky. Rather, their functions support life on *Erets*: they divide night and day, regulate times and seasons, and provide 'light upon *Erets*', a function which is specified twice (Gen. 1.15, 17). The larger light regulates light during the day and the lesser light during the night. By regulating day and night, the 'lights in the *shamayim*' also regulate time: 'signs, season, days and years'. The lights that emanate from the *shamayim* are created to meet the needs of *Erets!*

Some scholars argue that the word 'sun' (*shemesh*) is avoided as a polemic against an ancient Near Eastern deity who bears that name. It is just as valid, in terms of this narrative as a primal myth, to recognize that the emphasis lies on the basic function of these bodies as 'light–givers' for *Erets* rather than on deliberately negating any specific ancient Near Eastern rival mythology.

This regulation of the light is described at one point as 'rule over the day and over the night'. The verb rendered 'rule' is *mashal*, a term used for both 'ruling over' (Gen. 45.26) and 'being responsible for' (Gen. 24.2). Just as Abraham's servant was 'in charge of/responsible for' Abraham's household, sun and moon are responsible for/rule over day and night. The function of this 'ruling' is not to 'dominate' as the verb *rada* implies in Gen. 1. 26, 28, but to 'regulate' light for *Erets*. These lights are custodians of *shamayim* in the service of *Erets*, 'to give light to *Erets*'.

h. *Scene Six (Genesis 1.20-23): Water and Sky Creatures Emerge*
The waters are activated in scene six and water creatures emanate, including monsters (*tannin*) who have no prior existence as chaos forces as they do in other ancient Near Eastern traditions. As with *Erets* in scene four, the waters possess the capacity to bring forth all the living creatures that inhabit the oceans; the waters are partners in the creation process—a partnership that anticipates the ecosystems that we now know exist in our planet. The appearance of birds in the sky is not linked with any specific source—either land or water—even though the atmosphere or *ruach* might well be an implied source. The function of the birds is to fly above *Erets*, and across *shamayim*.

At this point in the narrative a divine blessing is introduced, a key factor in sustaining the creation process. To bless (*barak*) is to impart power. In this instance, that power activates a capacity to procreate and 'multiply on *Erets*'; *Erets* is the domain where this blessing/power is exercised and where the creatures involved find a home. The *Erets* myth depicts *Erets* as both the source of life and the habitat of all living creatures. The creation process continues: life is stimulated by the divine word, emanates from *Erets*, and persists through the blessing of procreation.

i. *Scene Seven (Genesis 1.24-25): Land Creatures Emanate from Erets*
The inner capacity and vitality of *Erets* as a partner with Elohim and a co-creator of life is made abundantly clear in scene six. A word from Elohim, and *Erets* 'brings forth' all kinds of fauna just as she brought forth all kinds of flora in scene four. The range of fauna includes cattle (domestic animals), all wild animals and creeping creatures (reptiles). The description is apparently intended to cover all species of fauna except human beings. The wild animals are specifically identified as living things 'of *Erets*'. In a traditional primal sense, they all belong to *Erets*. They are all 'Earth beings'.

Earth, *Erets*, is the source, home and habitat of 'living creatures'. As a life source, *Erets* supplies both the body and breath that create a *nephesh chayah*, an animated being or living creature. There is no duality here where the material derives from *Erets* and the spirit or life breath derives from God. All animated beings—except humans in this particular narrative—originate from *Erets*.

In a number of indigenous peoples's creation myths—sometimes called emergence myths—all life, including animal and human life, emerge or emanate from the land or sea and return there when they die. Typically, in Australia's Indigenous peoples's origin stories, animals and humans emerge from the ground as part of a sacred cycle of life. The identity of individuals is not only determined by virtue of their origin from the land as mother, but also in terms of specific places on the land where that person shares a common spirit with animals and ancestors. Earth is a spiritual source of life.

At this point I acknowledge my debt to Indigenous Australians, such as the Rainbow Spirit Elders, for my appreciation of the deep spiritual significance of Earth/land in the Bible, including Genesis 1 (Rainbow Spirit Elders 1997).

j. *Scene Eight (Genesis 1.26-28): The* Tselem *Myth*

1. *Genesis 1.26: The Council Decision.* We might well expect, given the progression of the plot in this primal narrative, that *Erets* would also bring forth that species we call human beings. The alternative primal narrative of Genesis 2 might also suggest such a development as a logical progression in the plot. In Genesis 1, *Erets* has been the key character, the valued partner and the co-creator with Elohim through scenes one to seven; *Erets* is the living source of fauna and flora. We might even expect, if we identify with *Erets,* that in the opening line of scene eight, we would hear Elohim speaking with *Erets* and saying, 'Together let us make humans'.

But scene eight introduces a totally new context and a radically different mythic orientation. Or, as Westermann (1964: 21) recognizes, from the perspective of *Erets* the plot is ruptured by a scene that stands in narrative conflict with what has preceded.

The new context is an unidentified location where Elohim confers with other beings and says, 'Let us make humankind'. The 'us' is reminiscent of the council of heavenly beings (*bene elohim*) in Job 1.6. There is no hint of this 'other' domain anywhere else in the narrative, nor that this is a created domain. Instead of calling on *Erets* to be a creation partner as in previous scenes, God addresses a totally new set of partners. The making of humans is a decision involving unidentified divine forces apparently from another realm. This primordial realm seems to be of a different character to the realm encountered previously in Genesis 1.

2. *Making a* Tselem. It is perhaps significant that Elohim speaks of 'making an image'. 'Making' suggests the concrete act of constructing a solid model or image. Like an artisan, it seems, Elohim 'makes' (*'asah*) a God-image as one would make a stone or wooden model. In several texts, the same verb is used for making concrete images. The Philistine priests, for example, give the order to 'make images of the mice' that are ravaging the land (1 Sam. 6.5; cf. Ezek. 7.20).

Interpretations of the *tselem* of Elohim (*imago deo*) in this Genesis 1 text are legion and cannot be explored in detail here. As we may suspect, a dualistic mindset has informed most interpretations in the past. A long tradition, that goes back to Philo who was influenced by Platonic thought, promotes the idea that the image refers to a non-physical dimension of humans: the mind, reason, consciousness or a spiritual core (Fergusson 1998: 13). The usual meaning of the Hebrew word for image (*tselem*), however, is something concrete and visible: a statue of a deity (2 Kgs 11.18; Dan. 3.1); a picture on a wall (Ezek. 23.14). Making a *tselem* implies making a figure like a statue. James Barr (1968:16) recognized a parallel between the action of God using an image to make a figure called a human and the process of Moses using a model or pattern (*tabnit*) from God to make the tabernacle (Exod. 25.40).

3. A Tselem *of Elohim*. In the numerous readings of this text, however, biblical scholars and theologians overlook the physical dimension of the divine action and discern a higher dimension in humans that somehow makes humankind creatures of a higher order. Traditional readings of the text foster a strong anthropocentric approach; these readings allow humans to play God by identifying with a dimension of God that they believe they emulate or express. In the October 2005 issue of *Interpretation*, Sibley Towner claims this text makes humans 'clones of God' and 'prime ministers of the King of the universe' but without the right to 'play God' (2005: 355). His reading is boldly anthropocentric. Dean McBride regards humans as the presence of God in the cosmos.

> The particular purpose of their creation is 'theophanic': to represent or mediate the sovereign presence of the deities within the central nave of the cosmic temple just as cult images were supposed to do in conventional sanctuaries (2000: 16).

Humans are beings 'made' in the *tselem* of Elohim. But which of the 'images' or portrayals of Elohim is employed in the formation of humans? If we assume a traditional interpretive approach that relates a key image/portrayal to its wider context, then Genesis 1 suggests a range of images/portrayals.

    a.   A nurturing life-force. The initial image/portrayal of Elohim in the primordial scene—where the wind of Elohim hovers over *Erets* in the primal waters—indicates a participating presence, a life force that is nurturing *Erets*. The probable birth metaphor may even suggest a midwife or parental image.

    b.   A verbal impulse. The second image/portrayal of Elohim is reflected in a creation process whereby the word from Elohim is an impulse that enables light and darkness to separate, the waters to divide, a firmament to be formed above the waters, and lights to be located in the firmament.

    c.   An empowering partner. The third image/portrayal that emerges is that of God cooperating with the domains of *Erets* to enable *Erets* to become a partner in the creation process by bringing forth all forms of fauna and flora.

In Gen. 1.26-28, however, a radically different image/portrayal is depicted, one that is not connected with the preceding images/portrayals.

d. A hierarchical power. The image/portrayal of Elohim implied in Gen. 1.26-28 is diametrically opposed to the preceding images which are essentially empowering. In this text, the image/portrayal relates to the transfer of power from a deity to one species on *Erets* who is given the mandate to exercise power over all the domains of *Erets*.

4. *Interpreting the* Tselem. Most scholars ignore the possible association with contextual images/portrayals and view this passage as clear evidence of the superiority of humans over other creatures. The *tselem* of Elohim, they argue, implies human superiority, and authorizes humans to rule an anthropocentric universe. The following quotations are representative of this point of view.

> The human was created by the special plan and providence of God. This indicates that the human being is a creature far superior to the rest of the living beings that live a physical life (Luther 1958: 56).

> The human is God's last, highest creation and is treated with particular thoroughness...The report that the human was created after God's image and that the human was given dominion over the animals explicitly expresses the special value of humanity (Gunkel 1997: 112).

> For the author of Genesis, the human has an incredible dignity, made in the image and the likeness of God, not as slave, but to have dominion over Earth (Vawter 1956: 43).

> The human, however, has from the very beginning been created for a task that sets the human apart from the rest of creation (Westermann 1964:20).

> The apex of the creatures is undoubtedly meant to be the human being (Renner 1988: 30).

> The dominion granted to humankind crowns the work of creation. The whole universe is centered on humankind, from the great to the small (Pietrantonio 1995: 68).

> The contribution of creatures, which God not only allows but indeed encourages, is clearest, and most decisive in the case of humanity, to whom God explicitly grants the status and role of the image of God and the commission to extend God's royal administration of the world as authorized representatives on Earth (Middleton 2005: 289).

From the perspective of *Erets*, it is apparent that interpreters have ignored the three preceding images of Elohim—the God who empowered *Erets*—and have adopted without question the hierarchical image that both overpowers and disempowers *Erets* and the creatures of *Erets*.

5. *The Royal Metaphor*. The function specified for the god-image creatures is 'to rule' (*rada*). Precisely because human beings are made in the *tselem* of Elohim, they are given the mandate to 'rule' all living creatures. Lest there be any question about what creatures are involved, the text delineates a

wide range of representative living things, including fish, birds, domestic animals, wild animals and creeping things. Humans are given the authority to rule as representatives of Elohim over all living things in nature.

As Towner points out, the logic of the text is clear: it reads 'Let us make humankind (*adam*) in our image, according to our likeness, *so that* they may have dominion' (2005: 348). Giving expression to the *tselem* of Elohim is not identified as evident in worship or communication with Elohim, but precisely in the function of having dominion over creatures. The logic is indeed clear: humans are created with the *tselem* of Elohim *so that they may rule*! That seems to be the essence of the *Tselem* myth.

There has been much recent debate about the meaning of the term *rada* variously rendered 'rule', 'have dominion' and 'take responsibility for'. Normally *rada* is what kings and taskmasters do (1 Kgs 4.24; 5.16)! Those who claim the text implies some sympathy for *Erets* soften the force of the verb by arguing that

- the term 'rule' reflects royal language;
- the first humans are thus depicted as ideal 'kings';
- humans, as rulers representing God, should reflect God's just rule;
- the ideals for God's rule through a chosen king are given in Psalm 72;
- this is interpreted as 'taking care' of the poor;
- 'ruling' *Erets* therefore means 'taking care of' *Erets* (see Dryness 1987: 54).

The problem with this interpretation is that a close reading of Psalm 72 reveals that *rada* is not linked with 'justice' or 'caring for' anything mentioned in the psalm. The relevant verses, apparently echoing the reign of Solomon, read:

> May he have dominion (*rada*) from sea to sea
> and from the river to the ends of Earth.
> May his foes bow down before him,
> and his enemies lick the dust (Ps. 72.8-9).

'Having dominion' in Psalm 72 means ruling over a domain in which all conquered foes have been forced to lick the dust. The royal metaphor does not temper the force of the hierarchical image. Ruling in the *tselem* of Elohim implies a form of royal domination that devalues *Erets* and the living community of *Erets*.

6. *Genesis 1.27: Implementing the Decision.* The implementation of the joint decision to 'make' humans in the *tselem* of Elohim is described in poetic language. The new dimension of this divine act is the designation of both male and female as bearers of the *tselem*. Both male and female humans bear the royal image and have the mandate to rule all other living creatures.

There is no indication of male rulers being superior in any way to female rulers; they are separated (*bara*) by sex but both bear the *tselem* that gives them the capacity to dominate.

Given the preceding analysis, it seems that the description of the *tselem* of Elohim in this passage

- is not to be interpreted from a dualistic perspective as a non-physical dimension of human beings;
- can be recognized as having an anthropocentric orientation that raises humans to a level above other living creatures;
- reflects the same terminology used in textual connections to describe making images for other gods or entities;
- portrays humans as visible, physical expressions of God's appearance.

As noted above, deities such as Baal were depicted by the image of a bull. Other deities had various animal and human faces that reflected their identity. In this passage, Elohim announces that a replica of this deity's appearance will be made in the human form. Just as Seth bore the physical *tselem* and likeness of his father Adam, so humans bear the *tselem* and likeness of Elohim (Gen. 5.1-3). And just as physical images of kings were located in various domains to represent the king, so also human beings are the images of Elohim located throughout *Erets*.

A further dimension of this action of God is discernible when we realize that the verb *bara* is used three times in this poetic verse. Following the research of van Wolde, we can render this passage 'God separated the human being made in his image'. That is, 'God placed human beings in a spatially distant position, namely, on *Erets*'. And again, 'God made a separation between male and female'. 'That is, God separated the human being into two sexes, each connected with its own sphere of life' (2009: 21-22).

By recognizing that *bara* implies physical separation, we can understand how, according to this myth, these creatures who look like God and bear the *tselem* of God are removed from that realm where other celestial beings like God may reside.

7. *Genesis 1.28: Empowering the Humans.* After humans have been made bearing the *tselem* of Elohim, they are empowered to carry out their role in the cosmos. This empowerment is described as Elohim 'blessing' the newly made humans. To 'bless' is traditionally understood as imparting positive power—especially the power associated with fertility (Gen. 24.60). Here, too, blessing imparts to humans the capacity to 'be fruitful and multiply', that is, to procreate and reproduce.

8. *Subduing* Erets. The blessing of humans is not intended to effect reproduction as an integral part of life, as with the other living creatures. Instead, humans are blessed *so that* they can fill *Erets* and subdue it.

The act of filling *Erets* suggests that *Erets* is the specific domain where humans are to rule. Fish may fill the seas (Gen. 1.22) but humans fill *Erets*, the domain where the *Erets*-born creatures already live. 'Filling' *Erets* implies a takeover. This is confirmed with the final mandate: 'subdue' (*kabash*) *Erets*!

The verb *kabash* has all the connotations of heavy-handed control. Zedekiah takes back those who have been liberated and 'subdues' them as slaves (Jer. 34.11). When Joshua completes the conquest of Canaan he is described as 'subjugating' the land (Josh. 18.1). In later texts, this verb is associated with the overpowering and rape of women (Est. 7.9; Neh. 5.5). The verb *kabash* connotes oppressive and harsh action and is consistent with the royal connotations of *rada* identified earlier.

In a detailed critical analysis of the *tselem* of Elohim in Gen. 1.26-28, Garr maintains

> *kabash* (subdue) is a harsh term that empowers, in this case, human beings to control, occupy, and subjugate a vast area by an exercise of mighty force. The 'image' entitles humankind to achieve decisive victory over the entire natural world. Stated differently, humankind will act like a victorious king over a conquered land (2001: 171).

In the *Tselem* myth, *Erets*, as the object of this harsh action on the part of humans, is the innocent victim of a royal ideology that elevates humans and devalues *Erets*. This portrayal of *Erets* is completely at odds with the character of *Erets* depicted in the first seven scenes of the Genesis 1 narrative. Elohim's partner in creating other life now becomes the victim of human 'subduing'; *Erets* becomes a slave of humans rather than their mother.

As if this humiliation of *Erets* was not enough, all her progeny are again declared to be the objects of human domination in the closing words of Gen. 1.28. From the perspective of *Erets*, humans are given the right to treat *Erets* and *Erets*-beings as inferior parts of creation: *Erets* is no longer a partner with God but a victim of humans.

It is perhaps possible that, as Gardner has suggested, the narrator of this verse reflects a hidden polemic against *Erets* as a power that 'nature religions of the surrounding nation deified' (2000: 24). But as Daniel Hillel, a *bone fide* ecologist, writes in an appendix to his work, *The Natural History of the Bible*, this text can be construed as 'a divine ordination of humans to dominate Earth and use every nonliving and living thing on it for their own purposes, without restraint or reservation' (2006: 242).

k. *Scene Nine (Genesis 1.29-31): Erets Provides Vegetation as Food*
The final scene recalls scene four in which the main character *Erets* brings forth vegetation, thereby demonstrating that *Erets* is not only alive but a partner in the creation process. In this closing scene, however, Elohim

does not specifically acknowledge *Erets* as the source of the vegetation but recognizes that the designated flora exists 'upon the face of *Erets*'. Elohim chooses to give all plants yielding seeds and trees bearing fruit to humans for food. Bird, animals and reptiles are assigned 'every green plant', that is, vegetation that does not have seed or fruit. This classification of flora may reflect a divine decision to give humans the more valuable species of vegetation for their food.

As earlier in scene three, Elohim 'sees' or views everything that has been created and responds positively. This action is not one of Elohim simply declaring creation to be good, but actually acknowledging that it is intrinsically good. The degree of divine celebration is emphasized by the verdict of 'very good'.

l. *Narrative Coda (Genesis 2.1-4a): Elohim Separates and Blesses Day Seven.* The ending of the primal *Erets* myth of Genesis 1 is a coda, bringing to a close the series of three separations and emanations described in the narrative. An *inclusio* links *bara elohim* in Gen. 1.1 and Gen. 2.3b and hence demonstrates the place of this coda in the narrative. As a coda, however, this passage appears to be located outside the sequence of creation events as such. But as Wallace has shown, 'The seventh day is thus part of the creation structure, yet it is distinct within it' (2000: 50).

The coda for the seventh day begins by announcing that the process of 'separating' the material universe—*shamayim*, *Erets* and their host—was complete, then adds that this process of completion actually takes place on the seventh day. So what happens on the seventh day to 'complete' the creation/separation process: God rests, blesses, separates, and sanctifies.

In terms of a typical primal narrative, the coda may summarize the completion of what is identified as incomplete in the primal setting. The cosmos is now complete and Elohim can rest (*shabat*) with creation. But that rest apparently does not mean inaction or taking a vacation: the use of *bara* in Gen. 2.3 indicates continued divine action. And, as van Wolde suggests, this verse means that God made the seventh day by 'separating' it and setting it apart of the other days (2009: 22). Elohim also blesses and sanctifies the day that celebrates completion—Elohim invests that day with a power comparable to the power of procreation given to living creatures of *Erets*.

If the creation process is alive on the seventh day to bring *Erets*, *shamayim* and all life to complete fulfilment, then creation continues (*creatio continua*). By the act of resting Elohim, as the impulse in the cosmos, relates to the completed cosmos through the act of blessing. That blessing, significantly, relates to the seventh day. Prior to that day, blessing has been dispensed to activate life as such. Now time is blessed with the inherent capacity to initiate, sustain, and restore life.

From the perspective of *Erets*, the concluding actions of God express both divine approval of the completed universe and continuing concern for the 'work' we call creation. The focus is not anthropocentric, but cosmic, embracing the completed separation of *shamayim* and *Erets* together with the celebration of divine rest! In a sense, the 'very good' that God experiences at the end of creation in Gen. 1.31 is now celebrated by rest, making it sacred and a blessing. Or as Moltmann writes: 'The God who rests in the face of his creation does not dominate the world on this day; he "feels" the world; he allows the world to be affected, to be touched by each of his creatures' (1985: 229).

As indicated in the Introduction, the use of the term *toledoth* in Gen. 2.4a is not accidental. It is part of the framing process that serves to link the initial *Erets* myth of Genesis 1 with the *toledoth* in subsequent chapters. The completion of the separation/creation sequence is announced in Gen. 2.1. The summation of Gen. 2.4a links this sequence with the specific 'separation of *Erets* and *shamayim*' in Gen. 1.1. It is possible that this sequence is viewed as comparable to the succession of human progeny indicated by the normal use of *toledeth*. In any case, by using the term '*toledoth*', the *Erets* myth is incorporated into primordial human history—and an anthropocentric framework is initiated.

m. *Sabbath Connections*

In the past, due to various dualistic influences, we have tended to separate God from time. Here, however, God is linked with time: blessing a period of time and thereby investing it with special power. God is in, with, and under time as God is in, with, and under the rest of creation. So, one dimension of time is filled with blessing, with life-giving impulses, with divine presence.

There are three textual connections in the Hebrew Scriptures that interpret the 'Sabbath' (*shabbat*) concept. The first, in the book of Exodus, is a social reading. Israelites should keep the Sabbath holy and rest from any work—'you, your son or daughter, your male or female slave, your livestock, or the alien resident in your towns' (Exod. 20.8-11). The reason given for this practice is that God did the same when creating *shamayim*, *Erets* and sea. Within the law codes of Israel, however, this practice was taken to the extreme, demanding that any who violated the Sabbath must die (Exod. 25.2).

The second reading, in the book of Deuteronomy, adds a historical dimension, associating this day with the liberation of God's people from slavery in Egypt (Deut. 5.12-15). On this day the people of Israel not only desist from work but celebrate their identity and freedom. Genesis 2.1-3, however, is not an aetiology for the Sabbath day as such; the noun 'sabbath' (*shabbat*)—as distinct from the verb 'to rest' (*shabat*)—does not occur in this passage. Genesis 2.1-3 is about creation, the domains of nature, and God's blessing of time on the seventh day; it is not about worshipping on that day.

The third reading, in Leviticus 25–26, relates directly to creation and to the land in particular. This passage is concerned specifically with 'a Sabbath of complete rest for the land', also designated as a 'Sabbath for the Lord' (Lev. 25.2-4). This rest is specified as a complete absence of any agriculture every seventh year. In the sixth year, the people of the land are expected to gather enough food to meet their needs during the seventh year. The focus of the Sabbath has moved from rest on the seventh day to complete rest in the seventh year. In the seventh year the land is to be made free to rejuvenate and restore its fertility.

A full appreciation of this process of Sabbath rejuvenation is only apparent when we discover that, in Leviticus, the land (*Erets*) belongs to Yhwh rather than to God's people who are named as tenants. Moreover, this land is explicitly designated Yhwh's sanctuary, that domain where Yhwh dwells, walks as he did in Eden, and expects to be kept free from any polluting idols (Lev. 26.1-2, 11-12).

The fertility of the land is dependent both on the faithfulness of the tenants and the rejuvenating presence of Yhwh. Total rest/sabbath for the land is specifically termed a 'Sabbath for the Lord'. The two are intimately interconnected. As God rested on the seventh day, so God rests and thereby rejuvenates the land every seven years. The rejuvenating presence of God is in the land, and by implication, in all creation. 'Land' in this Leviticus passage is the same word as *Erets* in Genesis 1—the former is a microcosm of the latter.

Accordingly we might well recognize a Sabbath principle embedded in this text: *it is vital for the rejuvenation of the sanctuary of Earth by the presence of God that Sabbath time be dedicated by human tenants on God's planet.* Or in more contemporary ecological terms: *it is vital for the internal rejuvenation/ restoration of the domains of nature that there be adequate rest time without the influence of external human forces that may have depleted a given domain.*

3. Retrieval

In the preceding analysis of the narrative we have retrieved dimensions of *Erets* as a character and subject that have not previously been fully recognized because of our past tendency to read the text from an anthropocentric or dualistic perspective. If we go a step further in identifying with *Erets* and reading in solidarity with *Erets*, we may be able to hear the voice of *Erets* behind the events. This articulation is a form of reconstruction which, I would argue, is as valid as scholarly reconstructions that seek to portray Genesis 1 as *Chaoskampf* myth, a liturgy, or a theological polemic.

In the following reconstruction of the narrative, *Erets* becomes her own interpreter. She tells the story from her perspective, a perspective we have retrieved through the preceding plot analysis of the *Erets* myth.

My Birth Story

I am *Erets*. In the beginning Elohim separated me from the rest of the primordial cosmos.

At first I was waiting deep in a primal womb. Everything was dark. Everything was enveloped in water. I had as yet not been fully formed or filled with life. I was just there, waiting. In the darkness, the wind of Elohim was hovering.

The first sign that things were changing for me was a voice in the darkness. Elohim called for light and separated the light from the darkness. Light meant life was coming. Light meant things could be seen when I emerged from the waters. Elohim named the light day and the darkness night.

The second sign that things were changing for me was Elohim talking to the waters. Elohim called for a vast canopy to stretch out high above. Elohim separated the primal waters and located half of the waters above the canopy and left me in the waters below the canopy. A canopy above meant that there would be space for me to be seen when I emerged from the waters. Elohim named the canopy Sky.

The third sign that things were happening to me was when Elohim spoke to the waters that enveloped me and summoned them to separate, to burst apart. Then I heard the voice of Elohim calling me to emerge from the divided waters and 'appear'. Now there was light, there was space, and there was an opening in the waters. Now I could appear, emerge from the darkness below, and be born. I appeared and Elohim named me *Erets*.

Can you imagine the honour of being brought forth personally by Elohim from the primal womb. Elohim was like a midwife. And my birth was amazing: I came from primal darkness into primal light. I felt very precious.

My amazing transformation continued when Elohim brought me to life in a new way. Elohim invited me to be a partner in the creation process. He summoned me to bring forth every imaginable species of vegetation from within my body. I became a source of life. I filled my surface with living flora.

No wonder Elohim looked closely at me and all that had emerged and said, 'I'm delighted!'

Now that the basic domains of the cosmos were in place, it was time for Elohim to fill these domains with appropriate forms.

First Elohim filled the sky with various kinds of lights to order the cycles of life and especially, as Elohim said, to provide light on me. Light was essential for the life I was nurturing. Light emanated from the sky to bless me.

Then Elohim summoned the seas to swarm with marine creatures and the air with birds. These creatures surrounded me and I sustained them.

Another special moment happened, when Elohim invited me to bring forth every imaginable species of land creature—mammals, reptiles and more. I was Elohim's partner in the creation of living beings. All fauna and flora emerge from me. They are my kin and I nurture them.

Again, Elohim looked closely at all that had emerged and said, 'I'm delighted!'

My Dark Story

I have another story to tell, a rather dark story about the origin of humans.

When Elohim thought about creating humans he chose to discuss the option with the council of celestial beings instead of with me. I was ignored and these other divine beings became Elohim's confidants.

They decided to create what are called human beings. These beings are apparently not my kin—they did not emerge from within me as other living creatures did. According to this version of the beginning, they are not made from the stuff of creation like other living things. Instead they are modelled on these celestial beings using an image of Elohim in the process. These new creatures apparently looked like Elohim and the celestial beings.

This action may have been reasonable if these images were formed to be my friends and work with me in nurturing life. Instead, they were given the special capacity by Elohim to multiply, completely fill my space, and dominate all the creatures that I had been partners in creating. All my kin were to be ruled by these images of Elohim. Why?

And as if that was not insult enough, these image creatures were given a mandate from Elohim to 'subdue' me as if I were a wild beast, an enemy, or a violent force to be controlled. By so doing Elohim discarded me as a partner and handed me over for humans to abuse. These image creatures not only looked like Elohim; they were given the right to play God in a cruel way.

Later, Elohim allocated the various types of vegetation to humans and all life on Earth so that I could nurture them. When Elohim saw the completed cosmos, Elohim said 'I'm very pleased!'

Elohim may have rested after the creation process, but it left me feeling ambivalent. I worked with Elohim as a partner throughout the process until the very end when a different kind of Elohim seemed to enter the scene and devalue me in favour of these new image creatures.

When Elohim rests, however, I am given time to rejuvenate. Sabbath also means a blessing is imparted to me and I will rise again, even if humans believe they are commissioned to suppress me.

Whether or not you hear the voice of *Erets* (Earth) in just this way, the task of reading the text from an ecological perspective suggests that we identify with *Erets* and explore the way this narrative would be read by *Erets* and the *Erets* community, of whom we humans are one species. As children of *Erets* we are invited by *Erets* to hear the stories from her perspective.

Chapter 4

GENESIS 2.4B–3.24:
THE ORIGIN MYTH OF *ADAMAH* AND *ADAM*

1. *Design*

Most scholars in the past discern that the structure or design of Genesis 2–3 revolves around the creation and fate of the first humans. While these designs are said to be viewed from a rhetorical or literary perspective, they nevertheless seem to focus on anthropocentric or theocentric themes. The rhetorical structure in five sections identified by Thomas Boomershine (1980: 33) illustrates this point.

    A. creation of the man and the garden (Gen. 2.4b-17)
        1. creation of the man
        2. creation of the garden
        3. river Pishon and land of Havilah
        4. other three rivers
        5. prohibition
    B. creation of the woman (Gen. 2.18-25)
        1. search
        2. creation of the woman
        3. union of the man and woman
    C. transgression (Gen. 3.1-7)
        1. serpent's interrogation of the woman
        2. serpent's interpretation of the prohibition
        3. transgression
    D. God's discovery of the transgression (Gen. 3.8-13)
        1. God's search for the man
        2. God's interrogation of the man
        3. confession
    E. punishment and expulsion (Gen. 3.14-25)
        1. curses of the serpent and the woman
        2. curse of the man
        3. notes of reconciliation
        4. expulsion

Two significant factors have generally been ignored in structural outlines such as the above: the genre of the narrative as a myth or origin story; the presence of a major character in the story—*Adamah*, the fertile ground.

Primal narratives such as origin myths articulate how realities of the human world are absent and come into existence. In this narrative, these realities relate to *Adamah*, the very ground/soil/land that the narrator knows as part of human culture. The narrative is a memory of the world 'in the beginning'. The following outline seeks to reflect these dimensions of the narrative as an origin myth.

Narrative Setting (Gen. 2.4b-6)
Primal Context
- *Adamah* without vegetation, rain or carer

Scene One (Gen. 2.7-15)
Primal Creative Acts with Adamah
- *adam* formed from *Adamah*
- forest grows from *Adamah*
- rivers flow from Eden
- *adam* to serve the forest of *Adamah*

Scene Two (Gen. 2.16-25)
Primal Relationships Established
- directive not to eat of the knowledge tree
- no partner for *adam*
- potential partners from *Adamah*
- woman created as partner for *adam*

Scene Three (Gen. 3.1-7)
Primal Enlightenment
- wise snake
- dialogue
- decision
- enlightenment

Scene Four (Gen. 3.7-19)
Primal Consequences of the Enlightenment
- fear and blame
- the snake crawls
- the woman in pain
- *Adamah* cursed

Scene Five (Gen. 3.20-24)
Primal Acts of Closure
- the woman named
- the man and woman clothed
- expulsion from Eden
- serving *Adamah*

It is typical of primal narratives that a primal lack or absence is announced at the beginning or during the plot of the narrative. In this narrative setting, a threefold lack is identified at the beginning: no vegetation in the fields; no rain; no carer for *Adamah*. By the end of scene one a forest is flourishing, rivers are flowing and *adam* is given the mission of caring for *Adamah*. In scene two it is revealed that the human has no partner. By the end of that scene woman and man have become one, united in partnership.

Scene three depicts a primal 'enlightenment' that affects the previous primal relationships and natural order. In scene four God imposes harsh realities on life outside Eden. As a result *Adamah* is cursed but *adam* returns to *Adamah* in death. In scene five the primal world of Eden is no longer accessible, but caring for *Adamah* remains the destiny of humans.

Our interpretation will both seek to avoid a narrow anthropocentric and dualistic orientation and to read with an appreciation of *Adamah* as a pivotal subject in the plot of the myth. The centrality of this character suggests that we, as Earth beings, ought to identify with *Adamah* at crucial points; and that we ought to ascertain the import of this narrative from the perspective of the fertile Earth. To facilitate this identification, we may locate ourselves in the habitat called Eden to appreciate its dimensions and primal ecosystem.

In this reading, the primal narrative stands on its own with a clear articulation of the primal absences, their fulfilment, and eventual modification, and the characters and plot of this myth represent a consistent independent plot. When we view the primal narrative of Gen. 1.1–2.4a as a setting or context for Genesis 2–3—as some scholars have done—the distinctive ecological dimensions of this text are lost, and above all, the radical conflict in ideology between the *Erets* myth and the *Adamah* myth is compromised.

2. Analysis

a. Genesis 2.4b-6: The Narrative Setting

1. *The Primordial World of* Adamah. The narrator makes it clear that the narrative is not part of recent history, but set in the primordial time when Yhwh Elohim made Earth and the skies. The setting is the world 'in the beginning'—a beginning quite different from that depicted in Gen. 1.2. The primal setting is a barren world: no life forms—except God—exist.

The absences in the primal world are identified explicitly as 'no plant of the field', 'no rain', and 'no one to care for *Adamah*'. The absence of rain is compensated for by an *ed*. While *ed* was once rendered 'mist', scholars now recognize that the term probably refers to a subterranean water source, as is suggested in the Akkadian parallel text (von Rad 1961: 75).

As Hiebert (1996: 37) demonstrates, the primordial setting also suggests an absence of agricultural crops; there is no 'pasturage' (*siach hassadeh*) and 'no field crops' (*eseb hassadeh*). Significantly however, God does not plant these forms of vegetation in Eden: they belong to the post-Eden ecosystem when rain is prevalent. The primal setting in these verses, it would seem, indicates absences in the primordial world before the ecosystem of Eden and the agricultural world known to the narrator.

A key factor in the primal setting is the absence of someone or something to *abad Adamah*. In Gen. 1.2, the focus was on *Erets*: Earth submerged in the waters and lacking any life or form (*tohu wabohu*). The primal scene in Genesis 2 is radically different: *Adamah* is not submerged in the deep but blessed with a water source from *Erets*.

The term *abad* has frequently been translated 'till'. Most translators and interpreters have assumed that the entire narrative reflects an agricultural orientation. The most frequent meaning of this common term *abad*, however, is 'to work, to work as a servant, to serve'. The term *abad* often refers to serving God or other gods (Exod. 3.12; Deut. 7.4). Sometimes the term does mean 'till' or 'work' the soil (as in 2 Sam. 9.10)—but given the fact that the so-called garden where the first human is first expected to *abad* (Gen. 2.15) is actually a forest, the specific rendering 'till' is unlikely (Newsom 2000: 64-65). Moreover, the coupling of *abad* with *shamar* (keep/preserve) in Gen. 2.15 suggests that this combination of verbs means something like 'serve and preserve' or 'care for and conserve'. Brigitte Kahl views serving as 'slave labour' and names *adam* the 'servant' of *Adamah* (1989: 54). The association with *shamar*, 'preserve', suggests that *adam* is the 'keeper' of *Adamah*—a role Cain later recognizes (Gen. 4.9)

In the Babylonian myth, the *Enuma Elish*, humans are made specifically to be servants or slaves of the gods; in the Genesis 2 myth, the service of humans is directed towards Earth and, in particular, to Earth's *Adamah*.

Before, during and after the world of Eden, *Adamah* is a central subject in the plot, and the source of life in all domains. More than 'arable' land, *Adamah* is the fertile soil; the mother ground from which humans and animals are formed; the source of the forest in Eden; the land that the first humans outside of Eden must work. Moreover, the forest planted in *Adamah* is located at some high point from which the waters arise and irrigate the surrounding lands.

The narrative setting identifies a primal need: *Adamah* needs to be served or worked. The plot outlines who is to 'serve' *Adamah*; who is to help in this serving; how the original mission to serve becomes problematic; and the subsequent need for that serving to continue outside of Eden. If we identify with *Adamah* as a character in this narrative progression, we understand the plot of Genesis 2–3 from a radically different perspective.

Does the narrative, then, also suggest an answer to the question of why God creates humans? I believe so. The primal setting articulates those dimensions of the natural world needed to transform the primordial scenario into the known world. And humans are explicitly identified as necessary to 'serve' or 'work' *Adamah*.

From God's perspective, the creation of humans might be an act of grace; from the perspective of Earth, humans are a basic necessity. Earth is not created for the benefit of humans: humans are created for the benefit of Earth—and, more specifically, to benefit *Adamah*.

The use of Yhwh Elohim as the name for God suggests that the narrator is clearly identifying the God who 'made (*'asah*) heaven and Earth' with the God of Israel. The narrative makes it clear, however, that this God is not only concerned with the origins of humanity, including the people of Israel; Yhwh Elohim is also concerned with the primordial and historical significance of *Adamah* as the domain that all humanity is expected to keep alive.

If we dare to place ourselves in the primal habitat prior to the acts of creation, we are located in a vast domain devoid of any vegetation, life, or waters from above. This is not a typical ancient Near East desert landscape with life forms and periodic rains; this is an image of *Adamah* as a totally barren domain, devoid of any vegetation and waiting for a living creature to take care of her needs. And this barren *Adamah* is a future mother.

b. *Scene One (Genesis 2.7-15): Primal Creative Acts with* Adamah

1. *Genesis 2.7: Adam Formed from* Adamah. The first action of Yhwh Elohim is to form *adam*. The reason for forming *adam* is identified in Gen. 2.15 where it becomes clear that *adam* was formed in order to 'serve' and 'keep' *Adamah*—a need explicitly identified already in the primal setting.

The intimate relationship between *adam* and *Adamah* is not only in terms of the purpose of *adam*; *adam* is also made from the very stuff of *Adamah*: the dust or dirt of the fertile ground. This dust or dirt, *Adamah*, is both the source of *adam* and the reason for *adam*'s existence. As Newsom states, 'we share common ground with Earth because we are common ground' (2000: 63): *adam* is an Earth being, like each of us—created from *Adamah* to care for *Adamah*, the source of all Earth beings.

The creation of *adam* is depicted as the work of an artisan or potter taking some soil from the *Adamah* and moulding it into a human form. The animation of this human form is effected by Yhwh Elohim breathing life into its nostrils. The term *neshamah* refers to breath: the air living creatures breathe (Gen. 7.22). As a result of this breath, the creature becomes a *nephesh chayah*: a living being. As a consequence, the first human created has this same basic identity as other living beings.

In some translations the term *nephesh* is rendered 'soul'. There is, however, no dualism of body and soul in this passage, and there is no hint of an ancient Greek conflict between body and soul. A human being, like other living beings, is *nephesh chayyah*, or *Adamah* animated by air from the atmosphere. This human is an integrated living being. The *nephesh* refers to a living being as a totality; each *nepesh chayyah* is animated *Adamah*—made of soil, air and water.

The term *neshamah* (breath) is often synonymous with the term *ruach*, (wind/atmosphere). As Hiebert demonstrates, the breath or wind of God is the atmosphere that surrounds this planet and animates all life (2008: 12). Psalm 104.30 makes it explicit that *Adamah* is brought to life by the *ruach* of God, the atmosphere that envelopes *Adamah* and all life. The divine *ruach* or *neshamah* is not some celestial intervention, but an integral part the ecosystem of Earth, the planet in which humans live. Humans are Earth beings—*Adamah* and *neshamah*, ground and atmosphere.

2. *Genesis 2.8-9: A Forest Grown from* Adamah. Yhwh Elohim plants a 'garden' in Eden. There is no need to seek a historical location for this site, although some memory of past domains may persist in the narrator's sources. Eden is an ideal place in the primordial world, a place where Yhwh Elohim also resides. The designation of this site as being 'in *qedem*' may suggest a location in the East; the term '*qedem*' may also carry the connotation of the beginning or the primordial time before known history (Prov. 8.23). Eden is a primordial place in a primordial time.

In Gen. 2.9 it is apparent that the garden is indeed a forest of trees, some of which are spectacular to look at and some of which produce food to eat. It is significant that these trees also emerge from *Adamah*. Humans and forests have a common origin and a continuing relationship: *Adamah* is a co-agent with Yhwh Elohim in the formation of both humans and forests; *Adamah* is God's partner in the creation of all life on Earth.

Two trees planted in the forest do not correspond to known species—'the tree of life' and 'the tree of the knowledge of good and evil'. No indication is given as to the nature and function of these trees. They are typical examples of plot anticipation—a clue that they will play a role in the fate of the forest and the forest creatures. Trees of this type are also typical of ancient primordial narratives or indigenous myths. In the primordial world of myth, trees, animals and other domains of nature perform acts that are not possible in the known natural world; the laws of nature in the primordial differ radically from those in the known world.

God's intimate relationship with humans in Eden is often noted. God 'forms', breathes', and 'speaks personally' to the humans. The same intimacy, however, is also evident in relationship to *Adamah*: God 'plants' and 'causes to grow'. Yhwh Elohim is God, the on-site landlord; human beings are his caretakers, created to work for and to conserve *Adamah*.

The narrator does not explore whether the first humans ate from the tree of life. The rest of the forest provided them with sustenance and a habitat. Clearly the first humans are created mortal, animated *Adamah*, destined to return to the *Adamah*. Yet, this mysterious tree provides a provocative alternative to the tree of knowledge which plays a key role later in the story. The narrator leaves us asking: what if the first humans had chosen the fruit of the tree of life rather than the tree of knowledge? After all, eating fruit in the primordial can have results that do not apply in the known world!

In the ancient Near Eastern legend of *Gilgamesh*, the hero locates the plant or tree of life—only to have the serpent steal it from him on his way home. This legend explains why the gods continue to enjoy eternal life, but mortals are destined to die. In contrast, access to the tree of life in the Genesis narrative is lost because God intervenes when humans disobey. Outside of Eden, humans no longer have access to trees of Eden that may have spiritual dimensions.

3. *Genesis 2.10-14: Rivers Flowing from Eden.* The narrator announces that a river flows from Eden, from the primordial world, into the known geographical world. This river presumably arises from the *ed* mentioned in Gen. 2.6. Waterways known to the narrator have their source deep in the primordial past and continue to provide sustenance for creatures living in the known historical world. For these rivers to flow into the known geographical world, they must be located at some high point, presumably a mountain. The location is not only the 'garden' of God but also the mountain of God: the source of living water. The identities of the Tigris and Euphrates are well known; the Pishon and Gihon probably reflect an ancient cartography.

These geographical markers make it clear that the waters arising from *Adamah* to meet the needs of the forest in Eden reach from the primordial past into the geographical present, from the ecosystem of Eden into the known ecosystem of the narrator. The *Adamah* of Eden is ultimately not lost: it provides water for the *Adamah* that humans outside Eden enjoy. Yhwh Elohim, moreover, is located at the source of the waters, recalling the abode of the Canaanite deity El, who dwells at the source of the rivers (*Baal* v 1-9).

4. *Genesis 2.15: Adam to Serve the Forest of* Adamah. The closure of the first scene connects the plot with the primal setting where there is no one to *abad Adamah*; it is quite clear that the role and destiny of *adam* is to *abad* and *shamar* the forest of Eden.

As explained above, *abad* normally means to 'work' or 'serve' rather than specifically to 'till'. The 'serving' function is clarified by it being in tandem with *shamar*, which means to 'keep', to 'preserve'. The role of *adam* is initially not to cultivate the soil, but to tend the forest trees and preserve them as both a source of beauty and of sustenance. The act of 'preserving' indicates a dimension of care that goes beyond 'working' or 'serving' in the forest. Preserving or 'keeping' the forest is a primordial task: *adam* is *Adamah*'s keeper! The call for humans to preserve old growth forests in our current environmental context echoes the very mission of *adam* to preserve the primordial forest of Eden.

The significance of these two verbs in this context becomes evident when we compare this mission of *adam* with the mandate articulated in Gen. 1.26-28.

Genesis 1.26-28	Genesis 2.15
adam has mandate	*adam* is commissioned
to 'rule'—*rada*	to 'serve'—*abad*
and to 'subdue'—*kabash*	and to 'preserve'—*shamar*

When located side by side it becomes clear that the verbs employed to describe the role of *adam* in Gen. 2.15 and in Gen. 1.26-28 are diametric opposites. As outlined in the previous chapter, the mandate to dominate incorporates verbs that are ecologically destructive, while the verbs employed in Gen. 2.15 are ecologically positive: the two traditions are mutually exclusive, in spite of the effort of scholars to harmonize the two under the category of 'stewardship'. In Gen. 2.15 *adam* is not a steward who rules on behalf of a king, but a companion or caretaker who 'serves' and 'preserves' God's abode in *Adamah* , the primordial forest of Eden.

The preceding analysis, I would argue, stands in tension with anthropo-centric approaches—such as that of Lacocque (2006: 86-88), for example—that contend that 'the human task is to "humanize" an environment which is initially uncouth'. Lacocque cautiously associates 'tilling' with 'taming' and 'keeping' with 'treating'. By introducing the kingship motif associated with the mandate to dominate in Gen. 1.26-28 and arguing that 'Adam's kingship consists in "humanizing" the whole of creation', Lacocque devalues the very *Adamah* from which *adam* and the forest emerge. Instead of recognizing the intrinsic value of all creation, he discerns within the text an intrinsic resistance in the created world that is to be overcome by human beings.

Traditionally Eden has been identified as paradise, a world where humans and animals live in harmony with God, with each other, and with nature. When we enter the forest of Eden described by the narrator in Gen. 2.15, however, we may find a somewhat different world, more like a rainforest with magnificent trees, some of which bear fruit—even without rain! From high in that forest, four rivers flow out to fertilize the world; deep in that forest God walks through a living world; on the ground in that forest, humans are the caretakers chosen by God.

c. *Scene Two (Genesis 2.16-25): Primal Relationships Established*

1. *Genesis 2.16-17: Directive Not to Eat of the Knowledge Tree.* The enigmatic knowledge tree planted in the forest in the garden is now forbidden territory. Why Yhwh Elohim plants a tree in the garden that could potentially cause death when its fruit is eaten is not clear at this point. There is an ecological network of trees that provide good food and appropriate shelter; the knowledge tree is not a natural tree; it is not a known species or part of

a recognizable forest. Why does God plant this tree? The narrator leaves us guessing, assuming it is the prerogative of God to impose conditions that limit human knowledge. The first directive or law of God in the Scriptures relates to a tree.

Eating of this tree means death, not mortality—from the beginning *adam* is made from *Adamah* and will potentially return to *Adamah*. Like the other creatures of Earth, *adam* is a *nephesh chayyah*, a mortal living being. The threat from Yhwh Elohim: immediate death for those who eat its fruit. No second chance, it seems! The expression 'good and evil' does not refer specifically to an ability to discern morally between good and evil, but an idiom that means more broadly 'knowing everything' about a subject: knowing the 'good and bad' or both sides the issue (von Rad 1961: 79). To 'know' good and evil may also suggest 'experiencing' realities other than intellectual knowing. Dimensions of that knowing through experience become apparent during subsequent scenes of the narrative.

The tree of knowledge is not 'the tree of death' as some have suggested—mortality is already a given. However, the tree does have the capacity to impart a level of experiential knowledge beyond that already given to human beings—and this is the temptation. The danger lies in disobeying God's command.

The divine directive is not associated with a sexual act, even though some texts seem to associate eating with sexuality (e.g. Prov. 3.20). In Gen. 2.16-17, the focus is specifically on the act of 'eating', a pivotal term that occurs numerous times in Genesis 2–3. The act of eating constitutes disobedience and the threat of death. The tree, like all other flora and fauna, has intrinsic value and emerges from the very *Adamah* of Eden. As a symbol, however, this tree represents the boundary between the human and the divine, and is the test of how humans will relate to their Eden landlord. To eat is to break the peace.

2. Genesis 2.18: No Partner for Adam. Until this point in the narrative, it would seem that Yhwh Elohim has been the companion of *adam*. However, *adam* has a role to play in tending the forest of *Adamah*, a role that he is performing alone. Yhwh Elohim chooses to create a partner for *adam* to assist in the performance of this role. There is no indication that this partner's role is any less important than the role of the initial *adam*: they are 'partners' in the service of the forest.

It is perhaps significant that this partner is called a 'helper', a term also used of God in the Hebrew Scriptures (Exod. 18.4; Deut. 33.7; Ps. 70.5). This lack of a suitable partner and 'helper' represents the final absence in the primordial world that needs to be rectified. The fulfilment of this lacuna will bring the primordial world to completion and establish the complete ecosystem of Eden. The 'helper' will be the culmination of this creation process in Eden.

3. *Genesis 2.19-20: Partners for* Adam *from* Adamah. Like *adam*, the living beings selected to be potential partners for *adam* are formed from the *Adamah*. They have a common origin and hence are potential partners. In this context, humans and other species are kin. The living beings identified here are 'every animal of the field' and 'every bird of the air'. The 'fish of the sea' are apparently excluded as not being like humans in some way and hence they are not potential partners.

This awareness of kinship with the animal world is common in Indigenous cultures—including Australia's first peoples—where specific animals share a common spirit with humans in a given community and with particular locations in the landscape of that community. In the forest of Eden there is no apparent alienation or dualistic division between humans and animals—they are Earth beings: kin and companions in the forest.

A scenario that is often overlooked by interpreters is the procession of species being led by Yhwh Elohim to *adam* for naming. Every animal—from mouse to elephant, from dove to eagle—is lead personally by Yhwh Elohim to *adam* for consideration as a partner. Yhwh Elohim is like a friendly game-keeper! There is a sense in which the initial *adam*—like subsequent genera-tions of human beings—names and thereby classifies creatures of the natural world in which we live. As we later come to appreciate, both *adam* and the animals are naked in this initial encounter, but not phased by their condition as they meet. They are all part of one naked family derived from a common *Adamah*.

Some scholars argue that naming in the ancient world is an exercise in sovereignty. The context of common origin and potential partnership, however, suggests otherwise. These creatures are kin not servants, potential partners not inferiors. Naming, in the biblical tradition, can also mean an act of acceptance and celebration. When Ruth gives birth to a son and hands him over to Naomi, it is the women of the village who name the child, not someone in authority (Ruth 4.13-17). To name is to know and to connect personally and communally.

In spite of searching the whole ecosystem of animals and birds for a potential partner, *adam* does not discover one that is just right. One final lacuna in the primordial world remains to be filled; that this partner is also called an *ezer*—often rendered 'helper'—does not imply a lesser being: the term *ezer* is used of God's 'helping' humans who cannot help themselves (Ps. 20.2). The partner is to help *adam* in the role of preserving the forest ecosystem of Eden.

4. *Genesis 2.21-25: Woman Formed as Partner for Adam.* The climax of the narrative describing the completion of the primordial world of Eden is the creating of woman. Yhwh Elohim does the work alone; *adam* is a silent and passive participant. Yhwh Elohim takes a rib and 'builds it up into a woman'. As a number of scholars suggest, the Hebrew word for 'rib'—*tsela*—may

be derived from a Sumerian play on words where the corresponding term mean 'life' as well as 'woman' (Schungel-Strauman 1993: 66).

The intimate interconnectedness of man and woman is made explicit in the response of Adam to the new creation when God 'brings' the man this potential partner. Though *adam* is made from *Adamah*, this partner is made from the flesh and bone of *adam*. Despite this apparent innovation in sourcing raw materials, the creation of woman confirms that ultimately the entire ecosystem of Eden is grounded in *Adamah*.

The equality and unity of man and woman is made explicit in the pronouncement of the narrator that becoming 'one flesh' is more important than commitment to the man's parents—a pronouncement made even before parents existed. Union for procreation is also vital for sustaining life in the world of Eden and beyond. Sex is already a planned part of the primordial world of Eden.

This primal pair is not characterized as young, virile or clever. Rather, they are depicted as naïve and childlike, unashamed of their nakedness. The primordial world of Eden is not only a closely interrelated family of living beings; it is also a world unspoiled by the habits of history and the subsequent knowledge of human experience.

5. *Interconnectedness in Eden.* These scenes in Genesis 2 reflect a perception of the natural world that recalls the principle of interconnectedness highlighted by ecologists in recent decades and explored in *The Earth Bible*.

As the mother ground of Earth, *Adamah* is the source of all life—connecting *adam*, human beings; the vegetation of the forests; the waters; and all other living beings. Humans are kin with the rest of the natural world and commissioned to serve and preserve it.

One element of this interconnectedness often overlooked is 'air'. All living beings are dependent on air for breath and life—and that air/breath/atmosphere comes directly from God. God is the atmosphere in Eden and beyond. This narrative points to the interconnectedness and interdependency of all creation, including God! If we identify with *Adamah* in this context, we gain a sense of her as a key character in the primal interdependence affirmed by this narrator: *Adamah* gives birth to a family of kin in cooperation with Yhwh Elohim.

This interconnected world of Eden is, however, not the real world we know. In Eden all relationships are apparently harmonious; there is no conflict in Eden. The potential exists for humans to eat from the tree of life and live forever in happiness. The Eden ecology is one of innocence and goodness. The two humans are ignorant of their nakedness and of any painful dimensions of this reality. Nakedness is natural!

In the following scene, the plot leads us from the ideal forest ecosystem of Eden to the real world we know. For the possible origins of the 'ecology of the garden' in the ancient world see Hiebert's analysis of the landscape of the Yahwist (1996: 52 ff.).

This memory of interconnectedness and kinship between humans and nature may be significant in the current environmental context. Ecological thinking has raised again our consciousness of interconnected ecosystems. The heritage of Christian theology, however, has tended to negate that sense of kinship and connection, preferring to focus on the concept of a 'fallen creation' and dualistic separation between humans and nature. Nature is to be harnessed as an alien force rather than embraced as a nurturing mother. Genesis 2 reminds us that we are indeed Earth beings with all creatures, and dependent on Earth for our being. The mission of Gen. 2.15 is a call to return home and care for the very source of our being: Earth.

d. Scene Three (Genesis 3.1-6): Primal Enlightenment

1. *Genesis 3.1: The Wise Snake.* The snake is introduced as that creature more *arum* than any other. In the primordial world of Eden other creatures are apparently also *'arum*, and capable of communication. The research of ecologists has made us realize that there are many modes of communication and awareness among the members of Earth's family—including reptiles (Goodenough 1998). That the snake communicates with humans is not identified as unnatural in Eden; the key capacity of the snake is this superior *'arum* nature.

It is preferable to name the snake a 'snake' and not imply sinister dimensions by using the alternative translation 'serpent'. The snake, like all the other animals, is an Earth being—born of the *Adamah*, the primordial source of all living things. Eden is not the domain of an alien character; Eden is the ideal primordial world where snakes and other creatures can speak.

The snake represents the voice of wisdom. The term *'arum* occurs elsewhere only in the Wisdom literature of Job and Proverbs. In Proverbs an *'arum* human being is astute, prudent, insightful and clever; the wise are *'arum*! Being *'arum* is the opposite of being 'simple' or 'naïve'.

> The simple believe everything,
> but the astute (*'arum*) consider their steps (Prov. 14.15)

The snake is an astute voice in the context of a world that knows only good and is apparently ignorant of another world that includes both good and bad. The snake, like Yhwh Elohim, seems to be 'in the know'. To declare the snake devious in any way is to devalue one of the children of *Adamah*. Wisdom sets the snake apart: the snake knows more about the ways of God than humans do and becomes the agent for revealing the truth (Howard 2008: 25). Some creatures, it seems, are closer to God in Eden than others— or at least they are wiser in the ways of God than their kin in creation. The snake is one such creature.

The snake's opening question, therefore, is one designed to challenge the 'simple' understanding of reality known to the primal pair. In Socratic fashion the snake asks the woman whether God has forbidden humans to eat from the trees in the forest, a question which she can answer and which leads her into further conversation with the snake.

2. *Genesis 3.2-5: The Dialogue.* The woman replies that all trees of the forest, except the tree of the knowledge of good and evil, are accessible. She repeats God's threat that eating will end in death, adding a personal rider that even touching the tree will have the same result. Essentially she speaks the truth about reality as she knows it. Her understanding, it would seem, comes by word of mouth from the man to whom Yhwh Elohim addressed the initial edict. But she is now caught in conversation with the snake who is wiser than human beings.

The snake responds by presenting another option to the meaning of the tree in question. The snake suggests four things will happen when anyone eats from that tree. First, that person will not necessarily die. Here the snake anticipates what, in fact, does happen—the primal pair do not drop dead, but experience the reality of a world where death is a recognized part of existence. The snake does not lie.

Second, the snake suggests that eating will lead to enlightenment: their eyes will be opened to realities previously unknown to human beings. This possibility makes the option exciting and enticing. The promised enlightenment is precisely what happens at the climax of this scene. Eating the fruit means taking the risk of seeing a world beyond the innocence of Eden.

Third, with eyes open to new realities, life is more than experiencing the good and innocent world of Eden. Life is now about knowing and experiencing both sides of reality: good and bad; pleasure and pain; life and death. Outside Eden there is apparently a radically different ecosystem and set of social values. Again, the snake does not lie!

Fourth, once these humans know good and evil they will become 'like God'. Efforts to connect this 'likeness' with the 'image' of God in Gen. 1.26 are counterproductive; these two texts reflect totally different traditions about likeness. If, as the text says in Gen. 1.26, humankind is already created in the likeness of God, eating fruit in order to be like God is not tempting! The likeness in Genesis 1 relates to power over nature; Genesis 2 relates to knowledge of nature. The potential to become 'like God' through eating of the 'tree of life' is explicitly negated by God in Gen. 3.22. Humans in this narrative never are 'like one of us', that is, 'made in the likeness of God'; they are Earth beings, not the 'God-image' beings mentioned in Genesis 1.

The four eventualities outlined by the snake in Genesis 3 come to pass. As God's admission makes clear (Gen. 3.22), the primal pair have indeed become 'like one of us' after eating the forbidden fruit. The snake, moreover, represents and reveals that wisdom which enlightens humans about reality and the knowledge that makes them 'like God'. The snake is the agent of their enlightenment; in wisdom terms, the snake is their mentor.

Subsequent traditions that identify the snake as evil or as the devil embodied as a snake reflect a dualistic world that is not consistent with the unified ecosystem of Eden. The snake may be astute and informed, but does not belong to another domain that represents evil. The snake is an Earth being, made from *Adamah* like all other creatures of Eden, including humans.

3. *Genesis 3.6: The Decision.* The woman's decision-making process follows a logical progression towards enlightenment. First, the fruit of the tree of knowledge, like that of other trees, seems like good food and worth eating. Second, there is something about the fruit that is appealing, suggesting there is another dimension to life, offering a new experience of reality. Third, and most significantly, the fruit seems to have the capacity to make the consumer 'wise'. We may hear an echo the wise words from Prov. 14.15 in her questions: why should I just believe what God says? Why not be *arum* and test the tree's fruit myself?

4. *Genesis 3.7: The Enlightenment.* As a result of eating from the tree, the primal pair do not drop dead; they experience a new reality: their eyes are opened. They see the world as never before. They know something about both the good and the bad, about who they are and what life means. They realize they are naked and must do something about it. They are no longer 'simple' and innocent; they are on the way to wisdom—they know something of the 'good and evil' that God knows.

The man and the woman now view the physical bodies they have seen many times before as objects of shame. What was once seen as pure and natural is now seen as shameful. 'Adam has imbibed of the knowledge of good and evil and now cannot help but see good—and evil' (Williams 1981: 277). We may question why God chose to plant this tree of the knowledge of good and evil in the garden. In the plot of this narrative, however, is seems to represent the means for humanity—and indeed all of nature—to move from the idealized world of the primordial to the real world of good and bad, a world only grasped and experienced fully and truthfully through wisdom.

Another dimension of this enlightenment is 'self-consciousness'. As human beings they become conscious of 'them*selves*' as naked. And, as Newsom points out, 'nakedness' as a concept can only be applied to human beings (2000: 69). The man and the woman become conscious of themselves as humans. Before their eyes are opened, humans and animals apparently lived together with no such consciousness.

This eye-opening experience, this consciousness of self as human, separates the man and the woman from the rest of created things—not in a dualistic way but in terms of known classification systems. Humans, who once lived in innocent harmony with all other naked creatures, are now clothed; they are now different, capable of shame. This new consciousness may well be identified as the birth of anthropocentrism and the root of ecological sin (Newsom 2000: 70). The ideal world of Eden, where all species live naked and in harmony, has changed: the post-Eden world of reality involves human beings conscious of their apparent separateness from the rest of creation from the moment of their enlightenment.

This text does not explore the philosophical question of the origin of evil, but rather the way humans come to know and experience the realities of good and bad in the known world. Evil is not 'already there' as part of creation in this narrative. The snake is not a subtle symbol of evil.

This narrative is about grasping life in the real world; the primal experience—through which this world is revealed, and *Adamah*—the good mother of all life, are part of both the primal and the known world.

e. Scene Four (Genesis 3.8-19): Primal Consequences of the Enlightenment

1. *Genesis 3.8-13: Fear and Blame.* The aftermath of having their eyes opened involves a subtle story describing how the first humans handle their new consciousness. Not only do they know shame and cover their nakedness; they now hide themselves from the presence of Yhwh Elohim. They are conscious that their relationship with their God is changed. A sense of guilt now accompanies their sense of shame: they seek to escape the divine presence by taking refuge in the trees of the forest.

The voice of Yhwh Elohim calling 'Where are you?' is innocent enough. God the 'forest ranger' is searching for human companions. The shock comes when the man blurts out his new consciousness: 'I was afraid! I was naked! So I hid!' Not only is Adam aware of his nakedness: he now experiences the reality of fear and the impulses associated with fear—something he apparently did not encounter even among the fierce wild beasts of the forest previously.

Yhwh Elohim then asks how the man has become conscious of his nakedness. These are innocent humans living in harmony with all other naked creatures. The answer is obvious: he has eaten from the tree of knowledge, the tree that enlightens and creates new consciousness.

Through their eating, both the man and the woman have become conscious of another capacity—the skill of blaming others. The man blames the woman and the woman blames the snake!

2. *Genesis 3.14-15: The Snake Crawls.* The consequence of the act of eating reaches beyond human consciousness to a process that transforms the ecosystem of Eden into a world where humans, animals and *Adamah* experience less compatible relationships. That process is presented as Yhwh Elohim pronouncing curses.

The snake is the first to suffer. In spite of being the agent of enlightenment for the humans, the snake has to face a curse that increases the separation between the snake and the rest of the animal kingdom. The evidence that the snake is cursed is the need to crawl on its belly and eat dust: a mark of humiliation and degradation. This curse seems to signal that the equality over creatures in the animal kingdom has been disturbed and that the animal world as a whole is no longer at peace. The decision of the humans to eat from the tree also has implications for the animal world. The humans sin and the snake suffers—it seems unfair.

Also significant is another violation of the harmonious ecosystem of Eden: animals such as the snake are now at enmity with humans. They will no longer live as friends in the forest, but do battle in the dust. If we dare to identify with the snake—as many indigenous cultures would do—the fact that the smartest of the animals must be separated from all other animals by a curse seems decidedly unjust. The snake was created that way, so why should it be condemned? Why should wisdom be downgraded in such a cruel way?

3. *Genesis 3.16: The Woman in Pain.* The woman's punishment for eating from the tree is associated with her body and her relationship with her husband rather than with the rest of the natural world. However, as Newsom argues, her pain in childbirth might also be seen as a manifestation of alienation from the animal world: she contends that of all creatures, only 'human females have such regularly dangerous and painful birth-giving' (2000: 70). The self-consciousness that comes with 'enlightenment' in Eden also involves a consciousness of pain and danger.

The cruelty of God's punishment, moreover, also extends to the woman's relationship with her partner. Here the narrator reflects a world in which the woman is now forced to express her relationship with the man as one of 'desire' towards him rather than communication as partners. The man, in turn, is destined—according to this narrator—to 'rule' over the woman: she becomes his slave! The ideal relationship of Eden is changed radically. Instead of being equals, the man dominates. A harsh punishment indeed! The mission of the man to 'serve' *Adamah*, the source of all living, is not reflected in his relationship with his wife, the 'mother of all living'.

It remains significant, however, that the mastery of women is interpreted by the narrator as due to the curse imposed by God for life outside Eden rather than as the natural relationship of equality between male and female evident in Eden. The memory of equality in Eden, therefore, persists and ultimately undermines the prevailing story of mastery of women in ancient history.

4. *Genesis 3.17-19: Adamah Cursed.* The third punishment is a curse on *Adamah*. In spite of the fact that *Adamah* is the source of life in Eden—the fertile ground from which humans are made and where the forest garden

is planted—and in spite of the mission of *adam* to 'serve' and preserve this forest garden, it is *Adamah* who receives the curse. Not only does *Adamah* give birth to *adam*, but like many mothers who suffer on behalf of their children, *Adamah* suffers. Nowhere in the text has *Adamah* been implicated in the actions that have provoked the divine curses; *Adamah* is an innocent bystander! Yet, by being addressed as one who is to receive the curse, *Adamah* is identified as a subject whose voice deserves to be heard.

The cruelty in this context is that *Adamah* suffers at the hands of Yhwh Elohim. This God, moreover, blames *adam* for the curse imposed on *Adamah*. By changing the way of life for humans from forest living to agriculture, Yhwh Elohim creates alienation between *adam* and *Adamah*. According to the narrator, the enlightenment of humans is translated by God into the devaluation of nature.

Instead of simply enjoying the fruits of the forest, *adam* must now toil in such a way as to produce 'field crops' in order to survive. In the process, *Adamah* will also produce thorns and thistles which will make agriculture more difficult. In fact, thorns and thistles thrive especially where soil has been disturbed. The fertility ecosystem of *Adamah* is upset by humanity's move into arduous agriculture.

The final verse of this unit is regularly read as an extension of divine punishment on *adam*. Life will be hard work until death! Death is the final blow!

If, however, we identify with *Adamah*, as Wurst has done, we may hear a different voice rising from the text. A close reading makes it clear that returning to *Adamah* is not an integral part of the curse, but a homecoming (2000: 99). As Wurst writes, the 'generous Earth-mother, who acted with God to produce humans, now acts to protect their precious creation' (2000: 100): *Adamah* not only wears the curse for her children—she also welcomes them into her arms in death.

Immortality is an option within the ecology of Eden. Outside Eden mortality is normal, and depicted as a return to *Adamah*. Job cries: 'Naked I came from my mother's womb and naked I shall return there' (Job 1.21). 'There' is a location in *Adamah*; as is the case in Eden, here—in death— nakedness is natural and existence is innocent!

f. Scene Five (Genesis 3.20-24): Primal Acts of Closure

1. *Genesis 3.20: The Woman Is Named.* Earlier *adam* as 'human' had named his partner 'woman' (Gen. 2.23) to emphasize the unity of their partnership. They became one flesh with one mission. Now the man, named Adam in the text, names his partner a second time: he calls her 'Eve'—a more accurate translation is 'Life'—because she is the potential mother of 'all living'. Within the post-Eden world of the narrator, Eve becomes the vehicle for perpetuating life through procreation. From an anthropocentric perspective,

Eve replaces *Adamah* as the 'mother of all living'; Adam seems to put his faith in the woman for the continuation of life post-Eden, even though he is earlier designated her 'ruler'. It seems that Adam moves beyond the narrow curse perspective of God and recognizes the woman, by naming her Eve, as his essential partner in procreation to ensure the future of humanity.

2. *Genesis 3.21: The Man and Woman Clothed.* Yhwh Elohim, conscious of human nakedness, chooses to further distinguish humans from animals by making clothes for the humans from animal skins. As a consequence, more animals become the victims of human knowing, and the tension between humans and animals increases. Though this action seems superfluous as the primal pair have already sewn fig leaves together to cover their nakedness, by providing skins of animals as clothing Yhwh Elohim seems to accept the reality of their new consciousness and assists them in preserving their dignity—albeit at the expense of the animals.

3. *Genesis 3.22-24: Expulsion from Eden.* The closure of the Eden segment of the *Adamah* myth involves a dramatic divine action that ends the ecosystem of Eden and heralds life in a new ecosystem outside Eden. We hear Yhwh Elohim reflecting on the situation with 'us'—presumably the members of the heavenly council. Now the fate of humanity is decided, it would appear, by forces outside the natural domains of Earth. The united family of humans, animals and God in the forest of Eden is now disrupted by divine forces that disturb the primal order of things.

The opening lines are a stunning admission that what the wise snake predicted has in fact come true. The enlightenment of *adam* means that humans have become 'like one of us, knowing good and evil/bad'. As indicated above, being like God brings to humans a new human consciousness with a level of knowledge that distinguishes humans from the animals and challenges the position of Yhwh Elohim in the forest of Eden. In the once harmonious ecosystem of Eden, there are now rival beings who are like Yhwh Elohim and who present a challenge to the role of God in the forest.

That challenge is made all the more ominous for Yhwh Elohim because if these humans 'like us' had eaten from the tree of life they would have lived forever as rival 'gods' in Eden. The tree of life is apparently the 'god-tree'; eating from that tree means not only being 'like us' but being one of us—becoming a divine being. Clearly, the first humans had not yet eaten from this tree; they were still mortal beings like all other creatures in Eden. Yhwh Elohim's solution: expulsion from Eden preventing any access to the tree of life, thereby marking a clear separation between the ecosystem of Eden from the world outside Eden. Bold mythical symbols of cherubim and a flaming sword are employed to block human access to the primal domain.

4. *Genesis 3.23: Serving* Adamah. Despite human expulsion from Eden, there is continuity between Eden and the outside world in the explicit connection between *adam* and *Adamah*: *adam* is to serve/work *Adamah* from which *adam* was taken. The mission of humans to 'serve' the Earth and the fertile ground called *Adamah* persists after Eden: *adam* remains *Adamah*'s keeper!

From the perspective of *Adamah*, in this continuity Yhwh Elohim tempers the earlier curse and recognizes that the primal bond between *adam* and *Adamah* persists. Whatever happens in Eden or outside Eden, *adam* and *Adamah* and their progeny are inter-related. Ultimately, *adam* was created to 'serve' and 'preserve' *Adamah* and that mission of humanity persists. In this narrative, humans are created to benefit Earth, not vice versa.

5. *Disconnectedness after Eden.* The narrative of Genesis 2 describes an eco-system in which humans, animals, forests, rivers and God are interconnected in an ideal and harmonious way. All of life is linked to *Adamah* and dependent on *Adamah*.

Outside of Eden, relationships have changed. Humans are enlightened beings 'knowing good and evil' but are removed from the primal forest. Humans and animals live in the same world, but experience enmity and conflict. Humans have a new level of consciousness that separates them from animals. Though *Adamah* remains the source of life and food, *Adamah* is cursed in such a way as to foster arduous agriculture rather than compatible forest life. Death after a life of hard work is now inevitable for humans.

The world outside of Eden is portrayed as decidedly anthropocentric. It is a world where the primal intimacy of all dimensions of nature present in Eden is replaced by conflicting forces. At the centre of this world are enlightened humans and a deity who accepts the new way of life rather than seeking to restore the original.

3. Retrieval

In the preceding analysis of the narrative we have retrieved features and dimensions of *Adamah* as a central character that have not previously been fully recognized because of a tendency to read the text from an anthropocentric perspective. If we go a step further and read in solidarity with *Adamah*, we hear the voice of *Adamah* behind the events and empathize with the injustice apparent as the plot progresses.

> The Voice of *Adamah*
>
> I remember the trees. I remember the harmonious ecosystem of Eden. And I remember the story they tell about how that system was disturbed and replaced by an agricultural age.
>
> I am *Adamah*, the fertile soil. I am mother ground. I was present before the experiment of Eden, the so-called 'enlightenment of humanity' and the

relegation of Eden to memory. I am the continuing potential source of life before, during, and after, Eden.

In the beginning, I wait to become an active life source. There is, however, no living being or force to activate my fertile soil. Then Yhwh takes some of my soil and forms *adam*, the first living thing, a human being. I am part of *adam* and *adam* is part of me. And *adam* is created to sustain me and vice versa. We share a common destiny.

Moulded by Yhwh from my soil, the human model of clay is inanimate until Yhwh breathes air into its nostrils. Becoming a living being involves effecting a harmonious interconnection between my soil and Yhwh's breath—the atmosphere that surrounds us all. That atmosphere is part of the life-support system in Eden.

Then Yhwh plants a forest in Eden where *adam* is to live and work with me in sustaining the ecosystem of trees—both trees bearing fruit and trees displaying beauty. That forest is also part of me, planted in me and integral to the ecosystem of Eden—but two trees in that garden do not correspond to species known in the world today.

From deep within the forest of Eden, a water source rises and divides into four great rivers that fertilize the forest and beyond. Rivers (not rain) characterize the water source of Eden, and forest (not field crops) characterize the vegetation.

Yhwh explains to *adam* the mission or destiny of human beings: to 'serve and preserve' the forest, to maintain the ecosystem of Eden and to celebrate both its fruits and its beauty; *adam* is appointed as my 'keeper'.

Yhwh also forms animals and birds from my soil. They are all my children, kin with all living things and potential partners of *adam*. Yhwh brings each species of animal and bird to *adam* to name and thereby classify them as part of the ecosystem of Eden. Both *adam* and the animals are naked. None of these creatures, however, are ideal personal partners and companions for *adam*.

Finally, Yhwh puts *adam* to sleep, extracts a rib and forms a woman to be an ideal partner for the man, Adam; Adam describes the woman as 'flesh of my flesh', a mortal being equal and united in the task of nourishing life. The storyteller speaks of them as one flesh, yet they are like children: naked, innocent and unashamed. They live together with the animals, who are also naked, innocent and unashamed.

The ecosystem of Eden is in intimate interdependence with my fertile soil; Eden's forests are the home of all living things, including Yhwh; a central water source emerges from deep within me; humans, birds and animals are made from my soil; humans are charged with the responsibility of preserving the forest; and the atmosphere which is the breath of Yhwh. It is an unspoiled ecosystem that I remember with wonder.

Then that harmonious ecosystem is disrupted: the snake, a wise creature made by Yhwh, 'puts the cat among the pigeons!'

The snake is neither fool nor fiend. The snake knows that if the humans eat from the tree of knowledge their eyes will be opened and things will never be the same in the ecosystem of Eden. They will be 'enlightened' like God, knowing the good and the bad side of things. The woman recognizes the potential for wisdom if she eats from that tree.

And she is right. But what she and her partner also discover is a new self-consciousness. They realize that they are different from the animals, a difference marked by an awareness that they are naked, ashamed, afraid, and ready to impart blame. They also realize they are mortal.

Yhwh could have accepted these 'enlightened' humans as part of Eden, but chooses to punish them for daring to disobey the command about the tree. That punishment spells the end of the Eden ecosystem.

From my point of view that punishment is unjust and unnecessary. Why should the snake, who is created wise by God and who tells the truth, be forced to crawl for the rest of his life? Why should the woman experience pain in childbirth because she now sees the world differently?

And, above all, why should I be cursed? Why? Why should I be treated as if I am guilty of some great crime? After all, I am mother ground, the source of life for all in Eden and beyond! I am the source of good, not evil. I know that sometimes mothers suffer on behalf of their children. But in this case, I am cursed so that *adam* suffers when they work with me. I am being used by God to make others suffer! This seems wrong!

In spite of all the suffering I may cause at God's instigation, I remain the source of life for human beings and I welcome them back into my bosom when they die. Death is a homecoming, a return to the very *Adamah* from which *adam* is formed.

In calling his wife 'Life' or Eve, Adam recognizes her potential to perpetuate life through procreation outside of Eden. Yhwh insists *adam* continues to be my servant outside Eden, working the soil to produce vegetation and food. Yhwh, however, is jealous of Eden and forces humans to live outside of Eden. Yhwh is even ready to kill animals to provide humans with clothes. Eden is closed off forever by celestial forces and the new age of agriculture outside of Eden begins. Eden is now but a memory of a primordial world.

The natural and social world outside of Eden is characterized by conflict between humans and other species; a consciousness that humans are separate from other living things; tension between living creatures; changes to the landscape caused by agriculture; an acceptance that death is part of the cycle of life; a greater sense of distance between Yhwh and the rest of nature.

My dream is that humans will not forget Eden, but work with the existing post-Eden ecosystem in such a way as to fulfil their original mission to 'serve and preserve' me rather than exploit and destroy me. The old Eden may remain as a memory but the vision of a new Eden is vital if I am to be sustained as Yhwh intended.

Chapter 5

GENESIS 4.1-26:
THE MYTH OF ADAMAH, CAIN, AND ABEL

1. *Design*

The structural design of Genesis 4—and especially the narrative within that chapter—usually revolves around the fate of Cain and Abel. However, *Adamah*, who is a key character in the narrative of the previous two chapters, is largely ignored in this model. The orientation of most interpreters is anthropocentric, with Cain as the villain and Abel as the victim. As Gunn and Fewell rightly recognize, God is also a character in the story—though not to be confused with a transcendent being of religious faith (1993: 28). Yhwh is present and active in the plot—but so is *Adamah*.

In the three scenes of this narrative, I would argue that the presence of a particular character informs the development of the plot: the presence of Yhwh, the presence of *Adamah* and finally the presence of Yhwh whom Cain associates with *Adamah*; Yhwh is not some distant being in heaven, but an active character in *Adamah*. It becomes clear in Gen. 4.14 that the presence of Yhwh is intimately associated with the presence of *Adamah*, and the character of *Adamah* plays a key role and represents the murdered Abel.

Though the latter part of Genesis 4 is part of the narrative framework of Genesis 1–11, it is a register of Israel's memory about one line of its primal ancestors rather than a narrative. Although the term '*toledoth*' is not employed, the language and substance of the text reflects a genealogy. The text also reflects the diverse social world associated with the Cain tradition whose descendants leave the agricultural world of *Adamah* and explore a range of other professions.

Narrative Setting (Gen. 4.1-2)
The Social Context
- Introducing Cain and Abel

Scene One (Gen. 4.3-7)
In the Presence of Yhwh
- Offerings made to Yhwh
- Yhwh accepts Abel's offering
- Yhwh counsels Cain

Scene Two (Gen. 4.8-12)
In the Presence of Adamah
- Cain kills Abel
- Abel's blood cries out from *Adamah*
- Cain cursed from off *Adamah*

Scene Three (Gen. 4.13-16)
Leaving the Presence of Adamah/Yhwh
- Cain's cry on losing the presence
- Yhwh's mark on Cain
- Cain's departure from Yhwh's presence

Framing (Gen. 4.17-24)
The Progeny of Cain

Postscript: (Gen. 4.25-26)
Compensation for Abel

2. Analysis

a. Genesis 4.1-2: The Narrative Setting

1. *The Primal Social Context.* The opening lines of the preceding narratives (in Genesis 1–3) introduced primal settings. Now, post-Eden, the narrator introduces two characters in a new primordial setting that suggests the beginnings of society. These two primal characters, however, are both sons of the first woman and man.

Eve's enigmatic comment that she 'created' Cain (*qana*) (cf. Gen. 14.19) with the help of Yhwh is the subject of considerable scholarly speculation. The narrator, it seems, wants the reader to connect the name of Cain with a relatively rare and similar sounding Hebrew word (*qana*) often rendered 'create'. Just how Yhwh, who remains an active figure on location in the post-Eden landscape, assists Eve in her 'creation' of Cain is not clear. Perhaps Yhwh is the first midwife in the Bible!

Abel, it seems, is produced without special assistance from Yhwh. No attention is paid to the meaning of his name because, as van Wolde points out, the meaning is obvious to the (Hebrew) reader. Abel (*hebel*) means 'vapour' or 'breath' in the sense of transience or worthlessness (see Eccl. 1.2). He is not the first born and therefore viewed by the reader as one who 'does not amount to much' (van Wolde 1991: 29). Abel is just another child—Eve does not even name him! Subsequently he is simply identified as 'Cain's brother'!

Also significant in this context are the specific roles that Cain and Abel play in this primal society. Abel 'tends' sheep and Cain 'works/serves' *Adamah*. These two roles recall the specific mission given to *adam* in Eden: to 'serve' and 'keep' *Adamah*'s garden. They are both, in their own way, fulfilling the original mission of *adam*, albeit in an agricultural and pastoral domain outside Eden.

As Hiebert notes, in this context there is no reason to assume any farmer–shepherd dichotomy in the mind of the narrator (1996: 39). Both Cain and Abel are living together on *Adamah* and both bring their produce to Yhwh. Yhwh resides in *Adamah*—and blesses *Adamah*'s inhabitants from this location. The area beyond this location—where Cain is later banished—is harsh and apparently devoid of any comparable divine care. Cain and Abel enjoy the ecology of fertile lands, *Adamah*: suitable for farming sheep and growing grain.

The primal world of *Adamah* in Genesis 2–4 seems to have a threefold structure:

1. Eden, the primordial place of origins—an ecosystem where all fauna and flora flourish and where Yhwh 'walks' with living beings;
2. a primal domain immediately outside Eden where Yhwh is also 'present' as a character and where humans enjoy the fertile lands for agriculture and pastoral pursuits;
3. less fertile domains beyond Yhwh's immediate presence where people build cities and pursue professions.

While this structure may suggest the beginnings of known society, the narrative is still set in the primordial world of myth where God is present in person, has intimate conversations with other characters, and acts to establish new dimensions of reality. The subsequent narratives in Genesis 5–11 make the primordial dimensions of this world very apparent. And in this mythic world, *Adamah* is an active character with a voice.

b. *Scene One (Genesis 4.3-7): In the Presence of Yhwh*

1. *Genesis 4.3-5: Offerings Made to Yhwh.* Long before any cultic guidelines are provided for bringing the first fruits of the farm to God as an expression of devotion, Cain and Abel are portrayed as grateful servants of *Adamah*. Here, as in Eden, there is an intimate connection between the human servant, *Adamah*, and Yhwh. At this point, there seems to be no obvious indications of the curse on *Adamah* that Yhwh pronounced in Eden. Later in this plot, however, the curse associated with *Adamah* that Cain experiences is so severe that Cain is no longer able to till/serve (Gen. 4.12).

Both men bring appropriate offerings from their productive fields to Yhwh. Neither offering is given any special cultic classification; both offerings are worthy products of *Adamah*. There is no clear indication that Abel is more prosperous than Cain. Nor is there any hint, as von Rad suggests, that Yhwh prefers a blood sacrifice (1961: 101). Yet Yhwh 'looks at Abel and his offering' but does not 'look at Cain or his offering'. Yhwh appears to be playing favourites. The reaction of Cain is one of envy and anger. Why? Apparently, because Yhwh dares to 'look at' Abel who would appear to be 'no one' as his name indicates?

If we consider the narrative using a Dalit (formerly known as 'untouchables' in India) hermeneutic—a point of view consistent with an ecological orientation—Cain is the powerful first-born child and Abel the less important and weaker one. Cain's name reflects his 'creation' connection with Yhwh at birth—he is apparently the child endowed with status and privilege; Abel's name means 'nothing' or 'no one'. In many cultures, the person who handles the sheep is considered polluted; as Gen. 46.34 states, 'every shepherd is an abomination'. As often happens in India, Cain the first born feels justified in killing Abel, the nobody (Deveshayam 1992: 9).

Cain's anger, it would seem, lies not in Abel's prosperity or superior offering, but in the fact that Yhwh dared to 'look on' this nobody called Abel and then to 'look on' his offering with favour. Yhwh seems to accept the underdog, the person considered inferior in society. It may also be noted that, ironically, Cain's role as a 'servant' of *Adamah* is closer to the original mission of *adam* in Gen. 2.15 than Abel's role of 'tending sheep'. Cain, the faithful first born who has been performing the primal mission, is furious that Yhwh should favour his younger brother Abel who is ostensibly nobody.

If, however, we read from the perspective of the flock—the *Adamah* creatures whom Abel is tending—we may discern an injustice. When Abel brings the best of his flock as an offering, this action apparently involves a killing or sacrifice. Abel offers to God the 'fat portions', a form of ritual worship normally implying the death of the animal and the preference of the deity for the 'fat parts' of the creature. If so, we may well expect *Adamah* to react negatively. The first act of violence, it seems, is not committed by Cain, but by Abel against his flock, living creatures of *Adamah*—and we might also expect the blood of the animal to cry out at this point!

In sympathy with *Adamah*, we may well ask why God would prefer an offering that represents an act of violence, rather than an offering that represents a faithful 'serving' of the ground of *Adamah*? Where is the justice in that? Even if Cain is unduly angry, from the perspective of these creatures, his anger seems to be justified. However, Abel's violence does not justify Cain's violence.

2. *Genesis 4.6-7: Yhwh Counsels Cain.* Yhwh responds to Cain's anger with an extended speech including four rhetorical questions. The first three are closely connected with Cain's angry response: Why are you angry? Why has your face fallen? If you do good, will you not be uplifted? These questions prepare the way for the final question in Yhwh's interrogation, the question that comes face to face with sin. This final question reverses the focus—the content is negative.

Sin is described as being like an animal 'lying down' or 'stretched out' at the door. This 'lying down' (*rabats*) may refer to the placid 'lying down' of domestic animals, or the threatening 'lying down' of wild animals such as a lion (Gen. 49.9). In this passage, the latter connotation seems apparent: sin is lying in ambush at the very door of the house, a metaphor that anticipates Cain's ambush of Abel (van Wolde 1991: 32-33).

The 'desire' of sin to be in control may reflect the language of Gen. 3.17 where the 'desire' of the woman is for the man, who in turn will 'rule' or master the woman. Here Cain is counselled to master or 'govern' sin in his life. The fallen face of Cain betrays his attitude long before he kills his brother—'sin' has invaded his life and Yhwh seeks to bring it to his consciousness. Unlike the choice of the first humans that led to a form of self-consciousness about reality, the attitude of Cain is exposed by Yhwh as an invasive force in creation that can overcome, or control, humans.

It is significant that sin is associated in this text not only with the figures of Cain and Abel as human beings, but also with their offerings, the products of *Adamah*. The primal relationship of humans with God is here closely connected with their labour, the produce of their labour, and the source of that labour. The identity of these primal humans is linked to their relationship with that domain of Earth that gives meaning to their lives: *Adamah*.

c. *Scene Two (Genesis 4. 8-12): In the Presence of Adamah*

1. *Genesis 4.8: Cain Kills Abel*. The brothers move from being in the presence of Yhwh where they made their offerings to a location identified as 'the field', a living expression of *Adamah* in whose presence the second scene takes place. The field of *Adamah* is also Cain's domain, the ground he works for his livelihood. The murder takes place in Cain's home territory. Whether Cain is aware of Yhwh's presence is not clear. Significantly, the narrator focuses on the environmental consequences that follow the murder and spends little time on the killing.

2. *Genesis 4.9-10: Yhwh Interrogates Cain*. In Eden Yhwh asks *adam*, 'Where are you?' In the field, Yhwh changes the focus to 'Where is your brother?' Cain is faced with a question about responsibility to his brother rather than his mission to 'serve/work' the fields of *Adamah*. Cain asks 'Am I my brother's keeper?' as if he has no responsibility for his brother.

As Swenson (2008) suggests, the narrator is reminding us of the original mission of *adam* to 'serve' and 'keep' (*shamar*) the forest of *Adamah* (Gen. 2.15), and the subsequent role of the *adam* to 'serve/till' a cursed *Adamah*. In that new relationship with *Adamah* post-Eden, 'serving' persists (Gen. 3.23) while the role of 'keeping' seems to have disappeared. Now it re-appears in a new form: humans have a role to 'keep/preserve' life—including the life of a brother—in the world outside of Eden (Swenson 2008: 36). In other words, Cain is saying, 'surely the firstborn is not responsible for protecting his brother who is nobody!'

The response of Yhwh is perhaps the most poignant and revealing text in this narrative. Cain is on trial and Yhwh asks 'what have you done?' Cain does not answer. Then Yhwh reveals that there is a witness to the crime and quite pointedly asks Cain to listen. Listen! There is a voice whose testimony is to be heard! Listen! There is a voice rising from a person you cannot see! Listen! There is a voice being mediated through the very *Adamah* whom you are supposed to serve.

The trial takes place in the presence of *Adamah* who enables the voice of Abel's blood to cry out with passion; *Adamah*, with whom Cain works each day, does not come to his defence. Rather, *Adamah* takes the side of the victim buried within *Adamah* who is crying out through the soil. The noun version of the verb to 'cry out', *tsa'aqa* (outcry), is regularly used to depict outrage at cruel acts of injustice: a great 'outcry' from Sodom moves Yhwh to intervene (Gen. 18.20-21); the great 'outcry' from the oppressed Israelites in Egypt leads to their exodus (Exod. 3.7).

'Blood' is synonymous with life—the very life and being that is dependent on *Adamah* for sustenance. Here the blood becomes the voice of *Adamah*. As Wittenberg (2000: 109) notes,

> *Adamah* appears here as a living organism which has 'opened her mouth' and has gulped the blood of Abel down her throat (cf. the identical phrase used in Num.16.30, 32; Deut. 11.6). Blood-filled it cries out aloud against the abomination of the crime.

3. *Genesis 4.11-12: Cain Cut Off from* Adamah. Yhwh's verdict relates not only to the future of Cain but also to the future of *Adamah*. His murder cuts Abel off from life on *Adamah*; yet he is returned to *Adamah* in death—albeit in an unsavoury way. Cain is cut off from *Adamah* because of the curse imposed on him by Yhwh. Kahl (2001: 63) notes that the

> first death in human history is not a peaceful receiving of dust returning to dust, but a desperate rearing up of the blood-soaked earth on behalf of the slain victim.

In Genesis 4, *Adamah* is depicted as a living character with a mouth that opens to receive the blood of Abel. Abel returns home to *Adamah* (as promised in Gen. 3.19) but via a cruel act of fratricide. In Gen. 3.17, *Adamah* was cursed and forced to make agriculture an arduous task. In Gen. 4.11, Cain is cursed 'from *Adamah*' suggesting that *Adamah* is not cursed in this text; however *Adamah* remains as the agent of Yhwh's action. Cain will no longer find agriculture merely arduous—it will be virtually impossible for him to get his living from *Adamah*. He is forced to be a fugitive on Earth. He is no longer a servant of *Adamah*, who has supported his life till now.

Cain's action effects his virtual alienation from Earth as fertile *Adamah*. When *Adamah* accepts/drinks the blood of Cain's brother, *Adamah* makes a choice against Cain, and Cain is alienated from Earth. As a consequence, *Adamah* no longer yields fruit when Cain 'serves/works' the soil. There is no home for Cain in his immediate world.

If the actions of the first *adam* led to the 'fall' of humanity into agriculture, the actions of Cain depict the alienation of humans from *Adamah* at a very early stage in human existence. Ultimately, in this version of primal human history, that 'fall' leads to the construction of cities (Gen. 4.17).

d. *Scene Three (Genesis 4.13-18): Leaving the Presence of Adamah/Yhwh*
Cain's outburst in Gen. 4.13 expresses the inner force of his alienation. His cry seems to be one of horror at the thought of life without either of the two characters he knows: *Adamah* and Yhwh. Isolation from his roots is a cruel punishment he believes he cannot bear. It means he will be forced to live in a world devoid of his life source (*Adamah*) and his protector (Yhwh). This cry is more than fear of the future—it reflects the reality that his deep connection with Earth has been severed.

Cain's explanation of his new consciousness is revealing. He declares that separation from *Adamah* means not only alienation from the soil he serves, but also from Yhwh, his god. To be driven from *Adamah*, he claims, is to be driven from the very 'face/presence' of Yhwh. When he connects the face of *Adamah* and the face of Yhwh, Cain makes it clear that the presence of Yhwh is not in the sky, a sacred site, or in a vague 'everywhere'; it is one with *Adamah*—the fertile land, sacred soil, and the medium of Yhwh's presence.

Significantly, when Cain leaves his place on *Adamah*, and dwells in Nod and builds a city, he no longer communicates with Yhwh. Understandably Cain experiences anguish about life in the wide world beyond *Adamah* he once served and God to whom he once brought offerings. And he fears that he might be killed.

Yhwh, who curses Cain's relationship with *Adamah*, now rescues Cain from immediate retaliation in the world beyond. He places a mark on Cain designed to protect him from attack and to warn would-be attackers of Yhwh's sevenfold vengeance. Cain leaves the presence of Yhwh but he lives under the protection of Yhwh's mark. Yhwh, it seems, is present in some sense in cities but not in the same way as Yhwh is with those who faithfully serve *Adamah*.

This scenes closes with a note from the narrator that Cain, by departing and dwelling in Nod, actually departs from the presence/face of Yhwh. The name 'Nod' is a Hebrew word-play on *nud* (wandering), used earlier to characterize Cain's new life (Gen. 4.14). The wanderer Cain lives in a town called 'Wandering'.

When the first humans are banished from Eden, they still live with *Adamah*; Cain is alienated from *Adamah* altogether (Wittenberg 2000: 170). Life without Yhwh's immediate presence in and with *Adamah* is recounted in the next scene.

e. *Scene Four (Genesis 4.17-24): Beyond the Presence of Yhwh/Adamah*

1. *Genesis 4.17: Cain Builds a City.* Once Cain is outside of the domain in which he experienced God's presence, Cain does not communicate with Yhwh. The narrator does not mention Yhwh even though Yhwh is a key character in the preceding scenes. And Cain no longer has any association with *Adamah*, the fertile ground from which he is banished. Cain is now in the world outside the immediate presence of Yhwh and *Adamah*.

In this world, cities are the first domain mentioned. Cain builds a city and thereby initiates a new social order that relates to Earth differently than the human beings previously associated with *Adamah*. Earlier, the name of *adam* is associated with *Adamah*, the fertile ground; the name Eve is associated with the source of life. Now, the name of Cain's first son is the name of the first city; the progeny of Cain have an urban identity rather than an Earth connection. They are 'emancipated' from Earth and alienated from *Adamah* by building a city (Wittenberg 2000: 112).

2. *Framing (Genesis 4.18-22): Cain's Progeny.* The genealogy of Cain reveals that his progeny are not merely city builders and dwellers: some are nomads living in tents—and distinguished from Abel who tended sheep on the fertile *Adamah*; some are artisans who construct bronze and iron tools reflecting their knowledge of using metals for human purposes; some are musicians, adept at playing the harp and the lyre. These 'urban' descendants of Cain reflect a range of developments in a 'civilisation' living without any specific association with Yhwh or *Adamah*.

These verses are part of a genealogical framework which provides a human context for this portion of the *Adamah* myth. This framing moves the reader from the primordial into the social and historical memory of Israel.

3. *Genesis 4.23-24: The Cry of Lamech.* The genealogy of Cain reaches a violent climax with the deeds and bold call for revenge by Lamech in his famous 'song of the sword'. Presumably a city king, Lamech is the prototype of a violent ruler. While Cain seems to have accepted his punishment—albeit with mitigating conditions—Lamech reflects an attitude of arrogant violence, boasting before his wives and challenging Yhwh to impose a vengeance on his opponents that is virtually unlimited, a vengeance not only on men but also on boys (*yeled*). The story of Lamech reflects the narrator's perception of violence typical of those who have abandoned the lifestyle of *Adamah*.

f. *Postscript (Genesis 4.25-26)*
In contrast to the people in the line of Cain, those in the line of Seth are said to begin calling on the name of Yhwh, the god whose presence is associated with *Adamah*. This 'calling on Yhwh' is the narrator's recollection of the origins of Yhwh worship, and seems to be independent of the offerings made by Cain and Abel.

Eve associates her third child Seth with Abel, the 'nobody' who was killed by Cain. Whatever the original connotation or geographical association of this name, this brief genealogical notation seems to be the narrator's way of offering some hope after the violent finale of the Cain genealogy. The name Enosh, the son of Seth, is a synonym for *adam* and seems to represent a new beginning for the human race on Earth. As Wittenberg (2000: 113-14) notes, the

> purpose was to create a contrast between two genealogies, the one starting with Cain and leading to the destruction of the flood, the other starting with Seth and leading to Noah and the future human race kindling the hope that the disastrous decisions of Cain—which broke all relationships, not only within the human family but with God and the Earth as well—would not be repeated.

Kahl suggests that 'Eve's narrative comeback in 4.25 marks the climax and reversal of the whole garden story' (2001: 68).

3. *Retrieval*

Based on the ecological reading outlined above and my efforts to empathize with *Adamah*, I hear the cry of *Adamah*. Another empathetic hearing of the voice of *Adamah* is that of Kristin Swenson (2008: 31-40).

> The Voice of *Adamah*
> I am *Adamah*, the fertile soil. I am mother ground. I was present before the experiment of Eden, the so-called enlightenment of humanity and the relegation of Eden to memory. I am the continuing potential source of life before, during and after Eden.
> Life after Eden was painful. Cain, the first born human whom Eve saw as a co-creation with *Yhwh*, was to succeed Adam and work with me, albeit as a caring farmer, a 'keeper' of life. It is sad that his brother Abel was viewed as 'nobody', as his name suggests, and remembered only as 'Cain's brother'.
> As appropriate in a caring agricultural ecosystem, I provided both brothers with the produce needed to express thanks to Yhwh, whose divine presence I house in my fertile soil. Yhwh, for some unspecified reason, looked favourably on Abel and his offering, but not on Cain and his offering. It did not seem fair! Abel had even killed one of my animal creatures in the process! Understandably, Cain, as the first born, was angry that his lesser brother should have been given special treatment.

Yhwh warned Cain to control his feelings and accept that knowing 'good and evil' in the world outside Eden also means learning to do what is 'good' even if things do not seem fair. For Cain was not only responsible for 'serving' me, *Adamah*; he was also responsible for 'keeping' my family, including his brother, Abel.

Perhaps Cain thought that out in the field where he worked he could do what he liked and no one would notice! But I saw what happened. I witnessed the murder; so did Yhwh. I absorbed the blood into my very being! I welcomed Abel back home, but not with the warmth I would have wished. And I refused to remain silent. I screamed 'bloody murder' and Yhwh knew the truth. I gave voice to Abel's blood and testified to Cain's crime. For Yhwh's presence is in, with and under me, the fertile ground of Earth.

'Listen!' said Yhwh to Cain. 'Listen to the voice of your brother rising from *Adamah*. Listen to the witness of *Adamah* against you. Listen and confess!' But Cain tried to excuse himself and claim that he had no responsibility to 'keep' his lesser brother. It was painful that the brother who was responsible for 'serving' and 'keeping' me chose to abandon me in such a cruel way.

Yhwh's response was just as painful. The curse Yhwh pronounced on me in Eden was painful enough: I was obligated to make working with my soil an arduous task for *adam*. Now I was expected to make sure the efforts of Cain were even more futile. I could not yield any produce, no matter how hard he worked. Once again, I suffered at the hands of Yhwh because of human misdeeds and I knew I would be alienated from this line of humanity well into the future.

Finally Cain understood! To leave me meant leaving Yhwh. To be separated from me meant being separated from Yhwh's presence. I am *Adamah* and I express Yhwh's presence.

Cain departed, abandoned me, left Yhwh, and became a city dweller!

Chapter 6

Genesis 5.1–6.4:
The First Inhabitants of *Adamah*

1. *Design*

At first glance, the focus of this unit is obviously the line of humans from Adam to Noah. Given the *toledoth* framework of Genesis 1–11, an anthropocentric orientation is to be expected. Nevertheless, *Adamah* persists as the habitat of the first genealogy of humans.

Many scholars associate Gen. 6.1-4 with the flood narrative that follows and read the events of this myth as further evidence of the disorder that provokes God to send waters of destruction. However, no specific connections are made with the flood event in these verses, nor are there any indications that the activities of Gen. 6.1-4 deserve the level of destructive divine intervention evident in the flood. The divine edict in Gen. 6.3 requires that human lives be reduced rather than that all creatures should perish. These verses are more like a postlude about what happens when the first humans multiply on the face of *Adamah*, than a prelude to the flood. This postlude makes it clear that the inhabitants of *Adamah* include long-living humans and Nephilim, the great warrior beings of old.

What cannot be ignored, however, is the *Tselem* myth fragment which is incorporated as a preface to this *toledoth*. Here the genealogy is linked directly to the *imago dei* text of Gen. 1.26-28. In Gen. 5.3 a neat transition announces that Seth, the son of *Adam*, bears the image of his father and therefore the *tselem* of Elohim.

The basic literary structure of this unit, taking these features into account, would therefore seem to be as follows:

- *Tselem* myth fragment (Genesis 5.1-2): confirms humans made in the *tselem* of God;
- royal *toledoth* (Genesis 5.3-32): the Seth line bearing the *tselem* of God represents the ruling genealogy on *Adamah*;
- *Adamah* myth fragment (Genesis 5.29): anticipated rest from the effects of the curse on *Adamah*;
- Nephilim myth (Genesis 6.1-4): story about the people who multiply on *Adamah* and their relationship with divine beings.

2. Analysis

a. The Tselem Myth (Genesis 5.1-2): The Image Confirmed

While the opening line announces that what follows is the book (*sepher*) of the descendants of Adam, the reader is immediately confronted with a summary confirmation of the *Tselem* myth originally found in Gen. 1.26-28.

This summary reference confirms several key features of the *Tselem* myth. First, these beings are specifically named *adam*, a generic term which becomes the name of the first human in the *toledoth*, Adam. It is also specified that they are the result of God's *bara*, a term which suggests a separation from God in some way as well as a separation of male and female (van Wolde 2009: 21-22). It also repeats the announcement that these creatures who bear the *tselem* of Elohim look like Elohim in some way, and that this image carries with it the blessing of Elohim so that these humans can multiply on Earth.

If humans continue to bear the *tselem* of Elohim and in so doing rule on Earth in the stead of Elohim, the subsequent genealogy may well be viewed as the royal line perpetuating the likeness of Elohim.

b. The Tselem *Inherited (Genesis 5.3)*

When Adam is 130 years old, he fathers a son whom he names Seth. As Cain is not included in this official line, he apparently does not bear the *tselem* of Elohim. Lest there be any doubt about this, the *tselem* is explicitly said to be present in this son of Adam, Seth. This son inherits the *tselem* of Adam who bears the royal *tselem* of God. In effect, the male line of Seth becomes the royal line, the line that perpetuates the *tselem* of Elohim. This royal male line represents the rule of Elohim on Earth.

If so, then this line of descendants has the God-given authority—much like the notorious divine right of kings in Western history—to multiply, rule over other creatures, fill *Erets* and subdue it. There is no comfort for Earth or the Earth community in God's recognition of this royal line. This line of humanity reigns supreme in the primordial domain.

c. The Royal Toledoth (Genesis 5.4-32)

Details of the royal line are minimal, giving only the age of the father when the first male child is born, the name of that child, and the life span of the father; only in the case of Noah are other male children of the ancestor mentioned.

There is precedent for such an antediluvian list of rulers in ancient Sumer and Mesopotamia (see Speiser 1964: 41-42). While the primordial patriarchs of Israel are not explicitly named kings, the association made with the *imago Dei* renders them royal representatives on Earth and 'rulers' comparable to their Mesopotamian neighbours.

The extended life span of these ancestors is not surprising. These figures belong to the primordial world of myth, before the realities of known history are fixed. The decree of Yhwh in Genesis 6.2 brings human lives more or less into line with the experience of known historical figures.

Details about the various ancestors outlined in this *toledoth* have been analysed by numerous scholars and will not be explored further in this reading. Suffice it to say that all those identified in this royal line—with the exception of Noah—are not associated with the natural world in any specific way; they remain rulers at a distance.

d. An Adamah Myth Fragment (Genesis 5.29)
Genesis 5.29 represents a poignant addition to the regular pattern of the genealogy and is probably a myth fragment from the *Adamah* Flood myth. Noah is singled out by his father Lamech as a potential source of relief for all those who labour working *Adamah*. The verb rendered 'relief' (Piel of *nacham*) suggests that work in the primordial world was arduous. The same verb in the Niphal is used to describe Yhwh's feelings about the humans inhabiting *Adamah* (Gen. 6.6). The concern of the narrator is that humans might find some relief or comfort in their labours made arduous as a result of the curse imposed on *Adamah*.

There is no corresponding concern for *Adamah*: an innocent victim of God's curse prior to the expulsion of the primal pair from Eden (Gen. 3.17). Nevertheless, *Adamah* might also ask for relief from the actions of members in the royal line if they exercise their right to 'subdue' Earth as an expression of their status as the image of God. The anthropocentric orientation of the text, however, suppresses the voice and rights of Earth— and especially of *Adamah*.

This verse, however, probably anticipates the post-flood decision of Yhwh never to curse *Adamah* in the future (Gen. 8.21), thereby fulfilling the hope of Lamech that through Noah relief would come. This *Adamah* myth fragment anticipates a return to the primordial world where *Adamah* is free from any curse that makes human 'service' arduous.

e. The Nephilim Myth (Genesis 6.1-4)
As demonstrated by Petersen (1979: 47f), Gen. 6.1-4 is a complete plot, even though it is summarized in four verses. The plot of the myth can be outlined as follows:

- Setting: among the people who multiplied on *Adamah*;
- Catalyst: divine beings take wives from among the women on *Adamah*;
- Response: God reduces the life span of humans on *Adamah*;
- Closure: Nephilim, progeny of divine men and human wives, also live on *Adamah*.

The plot begins by recalling the blessing of Gen. 1.26-28 which enables humans made in the *tselem* of Elohim to multiply on the face of the *Adamah*. These are apparently the humans in the royal line given in the previous chapter. In this plot, the listener to this ancient story may be surprised by a reference to daughters rather than sons of the royal line.

These daughters are described as *tob* in the eyes of a specific viewing audience. Throughout Genesis 1 most translators render this term 'good'; a much better rendering both here and in Genesis 1 would be 'beautiful'. This is precisely the term used by Moses' mother when she first sees her 'beautiful' baby (Exod. 2.2). What God saw, what Moses' mother saw, and what this new audience sees is something 'beautiful', a remarkable expression of creation's appearance. The text does not specify that the 'beauty' that appeals to the sons of God results from the fact that humans bearing the *tselem* of Elohim looked like gods and are therefore desirable.

The new viewing audience of these beautiful women of the royal line is the *bene Elohim*, usually rendered 'sons of God'. The various identities of these beings suggested by scholars is explored in detail by David Clines (1979). Given the primordial mythic context of these figures—where movement between domains of the cosmos is possible—and given the explicit contrast with 'the daughters of men', I favour viewing these figures as divine beings, members of the heavenly council (as in Job 1.6) and possibly among the 'us' who joined with God (Gen. 1.26) to create beings in their likeness.

Within the laws of a primordial world, these beings are capable of visiting Earth, marrying human women, and producing heroic offspring. While this capacity may not exist in the historical world, it is not explicitly denounced by God as wrong or improper in the primordial world. In that world, figures from the skies may apparently enjoy sexual relationships with women of *Adamah*. This breach of boundaries would, of course, not be considered acceptable—or perhaps even possible—in the known historical world.

The response of God to these sexual relationships seems unexpected. Neither the *bene Elohim* nor the women are addressed directly; rather, the life span of mortals in general is reduced to 120 years. Why? No explicit reason is given. Nevertheless, those humans who may have expected eternal life because they bore the *tselem* of Elohim, those humans who may have expected to live long lives as their ancestors did, and those humans who may have expected long or eternal life because of the injection of divine life through the *bene Elohim*, are now faced with the reality that human life would last no longer than 120 years. The eternal wind/spirit that animates human flesh would not be permanent in human flesh.

It is striking, however, that the party that violated the boundaries between heaven and Earth is not affected in any way. It is the humans, not the sons of Elohim, who experience God's response. As with the cursing of *Adamah* when Adam sins, a party other than the culprit suffers.

Clearly, the action of God confirms the mortality of humans and makes the close of the primordial era more like the real world of known history. Even so, the progeny of these inter-domain marriages persist after this divine modification of the laws of life. In fact, it seems as if God intervenes even before these half-breeds are born. These progeny are then specifically identified as Nephilim, legendary heroes of the distant past.

The existence of famous heroes and warrior figures who claim divine parentage is also found in other ancient Near Eastern texts. The Akkadian hero, Gilgamesh, is said to be two-thirds god. Though the precise connotations are unclear, the name Nephilim may also have negative connotations if associated with the noun *nephel* (abortion or miscarriage).

This myth also highlights the nature of humans in contrast to the Nephilim. The latter have a dimension of the divine that humans do not possess. Humans, however, are explicitly said to possess the *ruach* of/from Yhwh. In other words, the wind, air, atmosphere of the natural world is that dimension of God present on *Adamah* that gives life to humans: wind/atmosphere is synonymous with the breath/presence of God in Gen. 2.7 (Hiebert 2008).

3. Retrieval

Because this literary unit focuses on the human beings who live on *Adamah* and relate to divine beings from another domain, the role, interests and voice of *Adamah* are relegated to the background. Lamech alone is given a voice, complaining about the arduous nature of labour on the land because of the divine curse on *Adamah*. A voice of *Adamah* may, however, be retrieved if we identify with that precious domain of nature which is the habitat of humans.

> The Voice of *Adamah*
> I am *Adamah*, the domain that humans inhabit and where they multiply naturally through my blessings and nurturing. I am quite separate from the skies where divine beings allegedly live with God. The breath of God that surrounds and envelopes me animates all human beings.
>
> Because the genealogy of this narrative is linked with those humans who claim to be made in the image of God, I am conscious of the mandate they were given by God to dominate the natural world and subdue me under their feet. I am also aware of their orientation as rulers representing God, the creator king. And I remain angry that members of this line claim God has ordained life on Earth to be like this: that I am but a resource for humans rather than a partner with the Creator. With this royal line there seems to be no awareness of the reality that they are made from my clay and remain clay beings.
>
> And when I do get a mention, it is only a passing comment of Lamech who hopes humans might finally get some relief as they work on me, *Adamah*.

Their concerns are selfish; they have no empathy for me. I suffered that curse unjustly in the first place. And how they imagine Noah will be able to rectify the situation is beyond me.

What really disturbs me, however, is the violation of the boundaries between the ecosystems of sky and Earth. The story of divine beings having intercourse with women on Earth may not have been publicly denounced by God, but from my perspective it is intolerable. My domain functions with humans as part of the ecosystem of life. The intrusion of divine forces—other than the normal atmosphere, the breath of life from God—pollutes the system. The Nephilim are not heroes as far as I am concerned; they are aberrations that violate the natural world of which I am a vital part. God may well limit humans lives to 120 years, but God needs to prevent destructive divine forces from disrupting the habitat of humans and ultimately of all life on Earth.

Why should these divine beings get off scot free while the humans I nurture have their life curtailed? This dubious action of God reminds me again of how I was cursed for what humans did in Eden. Where is the justice in these acts of God?

As I anticipate the future, I wonder whether these ways of God on Earth will continue and whether my image as a victim of divine deeds will persist? Or will my vital place in the order of creation finally be recognized again as being as it was when I was first born?

Chapter 7

GENESIS 6.5-13:
RATIONALES FOR DESTROYING ADAMAH AND ERETS

1. *Design*

Scholars have long recognized that two flood stories have been collated in
the biblical flood account of Genesis 6–9. These two accounts have been
associated with the hypothetical sources or editors known as the Yahwist and
the Priestly writers (Habel 1988). When we re-read these two accounts from
the perspective of the victims of the flood event, rather different features
of these two accounts tend to surface. If we go a step further and consider
two central victims of the flood, we recognize that these two rationales are
probably continuations of the *Adamah* myth and the *Erets* myth identified
earlier. Two catastrophe myths continue the cycle of origin myths.

To highlight the two rationales given for the flood as continuations of
these myths, I have chosen to deal with these verses as a discrete unit in
this volume. In the first of these rationales the focus is on humans as the
cause of the crisis, but divine overreaction leads to a planned destruction
of all life on the face of *Adamah*. In the second rationale the focus is on
the corrupt ways of all living things, but the divine overreaction includes a
planned destruction of *Erets* itself (see also Habel 2006a).

First Rationale: *Adamah* Myth (Genesis 6.5-8)
- Crisis in creation: wickedness of *adam*
- Extent of crisis: all *adam* think only evil
- Divine reaction: Yhwh sorry *adam* was made
- Divine decision: Yhwh to blot out *adam*
- Divine overreaction: Yhwh to blot out ALL living on *Adamah*
- Divine afterthought: Noah finds grace with Yhwh

Interlude: Framing Verses (Genesis 6.9-10)
- *toledoth* of Noah

Second Rationale: *Erets* Myth (Genesis 6.11-13)
- Crisis in creation: corruption and violence on *Erets*
- Extent of crisis: *Erets* and all flesh corrupted
- Divine reaction: Elohim speaks to Noah about plan
- Divine decision: Elohim to destroy all *basar*
- Divine overreaction: Elohim to destroy *Erets*

2. Analysis

a. *First Rationale:* Adamah Myth *(Genesis 6.5-8)*

1. *Crisis: The Condition of Adam (Genesis 6.5).* In this continuation of the *Adamah* myth, Yhwh surveys the condition of *adam* and 'sees' their wickedness. These *adam*, who live 'on Earth', are very sinful—or as the Hebrew suggests, 'bad/evil'. Earth represents the habitat of humans, the place where Yhwh located them from the beginning, and is the source of their sustenance. They are explicitly identified as 'Earth' dwellers, but as verse 7 makes clear, the punishment relates to all who inhabit the face of *Adamah*.

The extent of human sinfulness is total: their minds are obsessed with wickedness. As the narrator says, 'every inclination of the thoughts of their hearts was only evil continually'. How *adam* became so completely corrupt in the primordial world is not explained; this condition seems to persist even after the flood (Gen. 8.21). This is indeed a pessimistic interpretation of the human condition: in ancient Hebrew the heart is equivalent to the mind! The first *adam* are characterized as obsessed with evil thoughts and presumably evil deeds. Yhwh faces a crisis in creation—*adam* now possess perverted minds.

2. *The Reaction of Yhwh (Genesis 6.6).* Understandably, this scenario causes Yhwh grief and anguish of heart. Yhwh, continues the narrator, 'changes his mind (*nacham*)' that he made *adam*.

Why is God upset? It seems the human experiment has failed! The special creature made from the clay of *Adamah* to live 'on Earth' has become a creature bent on thinking evil thoughts. Yhwh, who lived on *Adamah* with these creatures in Genesis 4, now finds life with them intolerable. As a result Yhwh 'grieves'—or perhaps, in modern terms—Yhwh becomes depressed.

The grieving of Yhwh over the plight of *adam* raises the question of whether there is a corresponding grieving of Yhwh over other domains of creation. Even though Yhwh feels justified in destroying other creatures on *Adamah*, does Yhwh also grieve over their plight? Clearly the perspective of the narrator is anthropocentric: in this text Yhwh expresses no concern for other creatures.

3. *The Decision of Yhwh (Genesis 6.7).* Yhwh decides to 'blot out' *adam* from the face of *Adamah*, their home. The implication seems to be that Yhwh has the power and right to eliminate a part of creation if it does not live up to divine expectations. One option would have been be to modify this model of *adam* so that they are not so obsessed with evil ideas. Yhwh, however, chooses the path of obliteration rather than transformation or redemption.

The narrative follows a logical and balanced progression to this point. The expected outcome of Yhwh's distress is that Yhwh will punish humankind—in this case by using a flood. There is, however, an unexpected development—a subversive dimension to the story that may alert readers to consider another agenda. Yhwh seems to overreact: Yhwh decides not only to obliterate all people on the face of *Adamah* because of their evil thoughts, but also the animals, birds and reptiles created with humankind from *Adamah*. In this plan, *adam* are beings obsessed with sin and must be cleared from their earthly home; however, the whole *Adamah* community is likewise condemned to oblivion.

Why? The animals and birds have done nothing wrong. The various living species of the wild are totally innocent. Yet they will die too. Nothing living on *Adamah* seems to have intrinsic worth in Yhwh's eyes. Yhwh seems to be obsessed with the *adam* beings and their ways. All living things are apparently disposable as part of the *adam* experiment. The narrator seems to be asking, quite subtly, what kind of God is this?

That representative species are finally rescued in the ark hardly exonerates Yhwh for killing all non-human life on *Adamah* because the human experiment is a failure. All fauna and flora of *Adamah* are relegated to oblivion because Yhwh is ready to obliterate one species—*adam*. From an anthropocentric perspective this may be considered merely collateral damage; from the perspective of non-human life, it is an unjustified divine overreaction!

This overreaction seems all the more striking when we recall that *Adamah* is not only the source of *adam* and all living creatures, but also the domain with which Yhwh's presence is associated in the earlier parts of the *Adamah* myth (see Gen. 4.14)—even though *Adamah* has been cursed. Is there a hint here that the grieving of Yhwh extends beyond the making of humans and also includes distress over Yhwh's chosen domain?

4. *Noah Finds Grace with Yhwh (Genesis 6.8).* The first rationale closes with a divine afterthought: Yhwh finds it in the divine heart to save Noah, even though there is no evidence to this point that Noah is different from the mass of evil-obsessed humanity. The selection of Noah is indeed, therefore, an act of grace and mercy on the part of Yhwh who is bent on punishment and destruction: Yhwh chooses to rescue one *adam* from the failed experiment called humanity.

b. *Interlude: Framing Verses (Genesis 6.9-10)*

1. *The toledoth of Noah (Genesis 6.9-10).* The *toledoth* of Noah serves both as a framing device to link the Flood myth with the preceding *toledoth* of Genesis 5 and to introduce Noah as the hero of the *Erets* myth version of the flood narrative. In the *Adamah* myth rationale, the potential rescue of

Noah is grounded solely in Yhwh's grace. In the rationale of the *Erets* myth, Noah is introduced in advance as a hero figure and identified as that one human who is above the world of corruption around him. Noah is hailed as an ideal human: he is 'righteous', 'blameless', and 'walks with Elohim'. Noah is the opposite of those humans described in the previous rationale.

c. *Second Rationale:* Erets Myth *(Genesis 6.11-13)*

1. *Crisis: Conditions in* Erets *(Genesis 6.11-12)*. In the *Erets* myth rationale, the portrayal of conditions is very different. In this scenario *Erets* is seen as 'corrupted' or 'spoiled' (*shachat*) and filled with 'violence' (*chamas*). The focus here is on the presence and role of 'violence'—or as Speiser renders the term—'lawlessness' (1964: 51). In the next verse, this violence is identified as a force that is 'spoiling' *Erets*.

The explicit reason why *Erets* is being spoiled or corrupted is not the sinful thoughts of humans, but because all *basar* has corrupted 'its way' on *Erets*. In this rationale, all life has also become corrupt in some way.

The enigmatic expression employed here is 'corrupting its way'. In the wisdom language of Proverbs and Job, the way (*derek*) of something is its driving characteristic, its essential nature (Habel 2003b: 286). The way of a hawk is to soar, spy, and dive from the sky; the way of the ant is to store up food for the winter (Prov. 6.6-8). Strangely, according to this version, humans are not being genuinely human, hawks are not being hawks, and ants are not being true to their nature as ants. The primordial ecosystem has broken down; violence fills *Erets*. The living creations of Elohim have all failed to live according to their essential nature or 'inner law'. Consequently, lawlessness abounds; creation is in crisis.

Again, an appreciation of the primordial mythic context is relevant. In our current ecological worldview, we cannot imagine all the life forms of the natural world simultaneously not being true to their respective bio-systems. In the primordial world, the current laws of nature may not apply—not only can divine beings have intercourse with human partners (as in Gen. 6.1-5), but any life form can behave in ways contrary to its very nature. Within creation there is such chaos that Elohim is apparently forced to take action.

2. *The Decision of Elohim (Genesis 6.13)*. One logical divine verdict, in the light of this chaotic situation, may be to start again by giving each creature a new 'way' that is not so easily corrupted. Elohim could transform all life forms so that they are true to their instincts, their inner nature. But once again, Elohim overreacts and the forces of divine destruction reach beyond the culprits to include the innocent. Elohim explicitly plans to destroy all these corrupted creatures 'along with *Erets*'. The habitat of all *basar*, *Erets*, will be destroyed with its inhabitants. As *Erets* is destined for destruction even though not the cause of the disorder, *Erets* seems to have no intrinsic

value; *Erets* can be annihilated willy nilly with the rest of life. We may well hear the voice of *Erets* asking why!

While the pre-flood worlds portrayed in each of these narratives is very different, they have one significant feature in common: the divine hand of destruction reaches beyond the guilty to include an innocent party. In the first scenario the innocent are the living creatures of *Adamah*; in the second it is *Erets* who suffers unjustly. We may well ask what kind of God is being portrayed here? Is the narrator also asking this question? (see Habel 2006a)

d. *Readings of the Rationale*

There are, of course, numerous flood myths from ancient and traditional cultures around the world (Dundes 1988). Three different Babylonian versions of the flood have survived. Details of these stories are clearly related to the biblical flood story. The rationale for the Atrahasis version of the Flood myth, for example, is human overpopulation and the associated plan of Enki is to solve the problem by limiting the human population by sending a flood. Other ancient and traditional Flood myths do not focus, however, on the intrinsic evil of humans as specified in the first biblical rationale, or on the problem of unrestrained corruption of nature as in the second rationale.

As Frymer-Kensky (1988: 67; nb the exclusive language is in the original text) points out, it is reasonable to link the biblical rationales with the subsequent introduction of 'laws' by which humans must live, the first of which is introduced immediately after the flood (Gen. 9.1-6).

> Genesis comes down on the *Leviathan* side of what is obviously a very old controversy about nature of man [*sic*]. Such perceptions of an inherently evil aspect of man's nature, one which is naturally prone to violent and unrighteous acts, logically entails a recognition that man cannot be allowed to live by his instincts alone, that he must be directed and controlled by laws, that in fact are a *sine qua non* of human existence. It is for this reason that God's first act after the flood is to give man laws.

The introduction of laws to curb human sinfulness and violence may indeed be a consequence of the flood, a way of dealing with the problem of human nature. The violence on *Erets* is clearly evident in the lawlessness among humans and other life forms. From the perspective of *Erets* and the *Erets* community, however, the divine overreaction—destroying almost all life as well as *Erets*—goes far beyond the need to introduce law. The two rationales for the flood are as much an indictment of the Creator as they are of creation.

As Clines (1998: 512) points out, for many peoples floods are one of the unaccountable natural catastrophes that occur; the storyteller's focus is usually how certain humans manage to escape. Clines recognizes a decidedly anthropocentric orientation to the flood narrative and contends that

the Hebrew setting of the Flood is fundamentally a narrative of God's dealing
with humanity, and the Flood is an expression of his will and activity...
his relationship to humankind is that of judge, to which function the legal
speech of sentence (6.13) corresponds.

It is significant, however, that in this biblical narrative, the sentence passed
by the judge falls on more than the humans identified as the accused.
The flood is more than punishment for human sin. It is a destruction of
the natural world and the existing order of creation: it is a return to the
primordial, and *Erets* also experiences the violent outcome of the judge's
sentence.

3. Retrieval

Given that this unit includes two rationales written from two different
perspectives, we may hear the voice of Earth reacting in different ways to
these narratives.

The Voice of *Adamah*

I am *Adamah*. I am the abode of humans who enjoy sustenance from my
fertile soil. Yhwh is also present with me, with *adam* and the rest of my animal
kingdom. In the mind of God, *adam*—created from my clay and filled with
divine breath to give them life—have allegedly become obsessed with evil
ideas. I don't know why they do not live as Yhwh planned.

This situation makes Yhwh quite distraught and I appreciate how Yhwh
feels. I feel the pain too. Surely something can be done to redeem these *adam*
and make them positive creatures who can live in peace with me and in
harmony with Yhwh. Yhwh is so upset, however, and plans to show no mercy
but simply obliterate all *adam*.

That upsets me too. But what upsets me even more is Yhwh's plan to
obliterate the rest of the living creatures I have been nurturing. I have been
their mother from the beginning. For Yhwh to do that is unjust and cruel.
Has Yhwh no sympathy for the living beings that enjoy life on my face, on
my landscape. Is Yhwh so callous that Yhwh can kill all life because of how
adam has behaved?

Or is the problem with the storyteller who has such a pessimistic view of
Yhwh that he interprets a story about a flood in terms of total divine judgement? The only divine goodwill the storyteller can find is Yhwh's willingness
to rescue Noah. Noah finds grace in the eyes of Yhwh—but no other person
or creature apparently does!

The Voice of *Erets*

I am *Erets*. I was the partner of Elohim in the creation of life in the beginning. Now, it seems, all life, all *basar*, has become corrupt and no longer true
to their inner nature. They do not follow the 'way' or instinct inherent in
their nature. So sad.

A divine sentence is passed on my world: my children are all violent
lawbreakers and must be put to death. The form of execution is a cosmic

flood. The verdict is painful indeed. Then I discover that I too must be destroyed along with all my children. As their mother, I am apparently guilty as well. Guilt apparently reaches back to the very first generation—to me!

Only one person, it appears, in all creation is faithful—a man called Noah 'who walks with Elohim'.

Elohim, the once compassionate Creator, seems to have been transformed into a heartless judge ready to annihilate all but a handful in creation...and me as well. The pain is almost too much to bear. Elohim seems to be so cold and distant, unwilling to find another way to resolve the crisis. Elohim chooses judgement as the answer, which means I too must be destroyed.

Chapter 8

GENESIS 6.14–8.19:
THE CATASTROPHE MYTHS OF ADAMAH AND ERETS

1. Text

In 1971 I published a volume entitled *Literary Criticism of the Old Testament*, although in retrospect it should have probably been called *An Introduction to Source Criticism of the Old Testament*. In that volume I attempted to separate the Yahwist and Priestly Writer's versions of the Flood myth that are merged in the current biblical text (Gen. 6.14–8.19). And while I may have misgivings about some of the textual divisions, I am still convinced that there are two narratives that correspond roughly to the Yahwist and Priestly versions of the flood story.

I include separate translations of these accounts based largely on the divisions in my earlier work in this chapter. By reading these separate accounts from an ecological perspective, however, two radically different orientations become apparent—a dimension that is apparent in my analysis of the two rationales for the flood given in the previous chapter. These two accounts, I have come to discover, are more than variations of a traditional legend—they are two catastrophe myths that have been integrated in the current biblical flood narrative and, at the same time, are continuations of the *Erets* and *Adamah* myth cycles found earlier in Genesis.

In the *Adamah* myth, the central domain/character of nature is *Adamah*; humankind is *adam*; the deity is Yhwh; and other living creatures are variously described. In the *Erets* myth, the central domain/character of nature is *Erets*; the deity is Elohim; and living creatures are designated *basar*. The first myth describes the removal of all life on *Adamah* by a flood caused by forty days and forty nights of rain. The second myth depicts a return to the primordial state where *Erets* is again covered by primordial waters.

The First Flood Narrative: An *Adamah* Myth

Rationale
And Yhwh saw that the wickedness of *adam* was great on Earth, and that every imagination of the thoughts of their heart was only wicked continuously. And Yhwh was sorry for making *adam* on Earth, and Yhwh's heart grieved. So Yhwh said, 'I will blot out *adam* whom I have created from the face of *Adamah*, humans and beasts, creeping things and birds of the air, because I am sorry that

I made them'. But Noah found grace in the eyes of Yhwh.

Decision to Save Species
So Yhwh said to Noah, 'Go aboard the ark, you and all your household, for I have seen that you are righteous before me in this generation. Take with you seven pairs of all clean animals, the male and his mate, and one pair of the animals that are not clean, the male and his mate. Also from the birds of the sky seven pair, male and female, to keep their seed alive upon the face of Earth. For in seven days time I will cause it to rain upon Earth 40 days and 40 nights, and I will blot out everything animated which I made from the face of *Adamah*.' So Noah did just as Yhwh commanded him.

Advent of the Flood
Then Noah and his sons and his wife boarded the ark to escape the waters of the flood. From the clean animals and the animals that are not clean, and from the birds and from everything that creeps on the ground (they boarded).
     After seven days the waters of the flood came upon Earth. And rain fell upon Earth 40 days and 40 nights. And Yhwh shut him (Noah) in.

Extent of the Flood
And there was a flood upon Earth for 40 days. And the waters increased and lifted the ark and it rose above Earth. Everything on the dry land with the breath of life in its nostrils died. He blotted out everything animated which was on the face of *Adamah*, both human and beast, creeping things and birds of the sky. They were blotted out from Earth. Only Noah was left and those that were with him in the ark.

Termination of the Flood
Then the rain was restrained from the sky and the waters receded from Earth continually. At the end of 40 days Noah opened the window of the ark which he had made and he sent forth a raven. It went to and fro until the waters were dried up from Earth. Then he sent forth a dove from him, to see if the waters had subsided from the face of *Adamah*. But the dove found no resting place for her foot, so she returned to him in the ark, for the waters were still upon the face of Earth. And he stretched forth his hand and took her and brought her into the ark with him. He waited another seven days and again he sent forth the dove out of the ark. And the dove came back to him in the evening, and lo, a freshly picked olive branch. So Noah knew the waters had subsided from Earth. Then he waited another seven days and sent forth the dove and she did not return to him anymore. So Noah removed the covering of the ark, and looked and behold the face of *Adamah* was dry.

The Second Flood Narrative: an *Erets* Myth

Rationale
Noah was a righteous man, blameless among his contemporaries. And Noah walked with Elohim. And Noah had three sons, Shem, Ham and Japheth. And *Erets* grew corrupt before Elohim. And *Erets* was full of violence. And Elohim saw *Erets* and behold it was corrupt, for all *basar* had corrupted its way on *Erets*. And Elohim said to Noah, 'I have determined to make an end of all *basar*, for *Erets* is filled with violence through them and behold I will annihilate (corrupt) them with *Erets*'.

Decision to Save Species

'Make yourself an ark of resinous wood. Make it with reeds and cover it with pitch inside and out. This is how you are to make it: the length of the ark 300 cubits, its breadth 50 cubits and its height 30 cubits. Make a roof for the ark and finish it to a cubit above, and set the door of the ark on the side; make it with the first, second and third decks.

For my part, I am bringing the flood of waters upon *Erets* to annihilate (corrupt) all *basar* in which is the breath of life under the sky. But I will establish my covenant with you, and you shall go on board the ark, you, your sons, your wife, and your son's wives along with you.

And from every living thing of all *basar*, two of each sort you shall bring aboard the ark, to save their lives with yours; they must be male and female. From the birds according to their kind, from every creeping thing of the ground, according to its kind, two of every sort shall come in to you to keep them alive. And take with you every sort of food which is eaten and store it, and it shall serve for food for you and them.'

So Noah did just as Elohim had commanded him. So he did.

Advent of the Flood

And Noah was 600 years old when the flood of waters came upon *Erets*. Two of each kind boarded the ark with Noah, male and female, as God had commanded Noah.

In the 600th year of Noah's life, in the 2nd month, on the 17th day of the month, on the very day, all the fountains of the great deep burst forth and the windows of heaven opened. On the very same day, Noah and his sons, Shem, Ham and Japheth, and Noah's wife and the three wives of his sons with them, boarded the ark, they and every beast according to its kind and all the cattle according to their kinds, and everything that creeps on *Erets* according to its kind and every bird according to its kind, every bird of every sort. They boarded the ark with Noah, two and two of all *basar* in which there was the breath of life. And those who boarded, male and female from all *basar*, entered as Elohim had commanded him.

Extent of the Flood

The flood waters prevailed and increased greatly, and the ark went upon the face of the waters. And the waters prevailed exceedingly upon *Erets* and covered all the high mountains which are under all the skies. The waters prevailed above the mountains, covering them fifteen cubits deep. And all *basar* expired that moved on *Erets*, birds, cattle, beasts, all swarming creatures who swarm on *Erets* and every human. And the waters prevailed upon *Erets* 150 days.

Termination of the Flood

Then Elohim remembered Noah and all the beasts and all the cattle that were with him in the ark. And Elohim made a wind blow on *Erets* and the waters subsided. And the fountains of the deep and the windows of skies were closed. At the end of 150 days the waters had abated. And in the 7th month, on the 17th day of the month, the ark came to rest on the mountains of Ararat. And the waters continued to abate until the 10th month; and in the 10th month, the 1st day of the month, the tops of the mountains were seen. In the 601st year, in the 1st month, on the 1st day of the month, the waters were dried up from *Erets*. In 2nd month, on the 27th day of the month, *Erets* was dry.

Then Elohim ordered Noah: 'Go out from the ark, you and your wife and your sons's wives with you. Bring forth with you every living thing that is with you of all *basar*—birds and animals and every creeping thing that creeps on *Erets*—that they may breed abundantly and be fruitful and multiply on *Erets*.' So Noah went forth, and his sons and his wife and his sons's wives with him. And every beast, every creeping thing, and every bird, everything that moves upon *Erets*, went forth by families out of the ark.

2. Design

	The *Adamah* Flood Myth	The *Erets* Flood Myth
Rationale for the Flood		
Situation:	Great wickedness of *adam*	All *basar* with corrupted ways
Divine Reaction:	Yhwh sorry	Elohim communicates with Noah
Divine Decision:	Yhwh to blot out *adam*	Elohim to destroy all *basar*
Overreaction:	To blot out all on *Adamah*	Elohim to destroy *Erets*
Divine Afterthought:	Noah finds grace	Noah found righteous
Decision to Save Species		
Concerning the Ark:	Noah to enter ark	Noah to make ark as specified
Species Specified:	7 clean, 2 unclean	2 of each kind
Reason Given:	To keep seed alive	Covenant with Noah to keep alive
Extent of the Flood:	Blot out life on *Adamah*	Destroy all *basar* under the sky
Advent of the Flood		
Boarding of ark:	Noah and animals board	Noah, family, 2 of each kind
Date of the Flood:		17.2.600 of Noah's life
Source of the Flood:	40 days and nights of rain	Fountains of deep and windows of sky
Extent of the Flood		
Flooding:	On Earth 40 days	Mighty waters for 150 days
Extent:	Lifts ark above Earth	Rises 15 cubits above mountains
Species:	All life on *Adamah* dies	All *basar* on *Erets* expires
Termination of the Flood		
Timing:	At end of 40 days	At end of 150 days
Cause:	Rains cease from sky closed	Wind blows on *Erets*, fountains and windows
Evidence of end:	Noah sends dove and raven	Ark rests on mountains of Ararat
Closing scenario:	Dove does not return	Animals depart to multiply
After the Flood:	Noah sees *Adamah* is dry	Noah and family leave ark
Date of closure:		27.2.601 of Noah's life

3. *Analysis*

a. *The First* (Adamah) *Flood Myth*

1. *Introduction.* This analysis does not make a detailed comparison with famous flood narratives of ancient Babylon or elsewhere in ancient or indigenous cultures, regardless of how similar they are (Dundes 1988), or discuss locations where archaeological relics resulting from floods have been found by archaeologists.

My concern is to discern those domains, characters and voices in the text that have been ignored—largely because of the anthropocentric readings of scholars in which the figure of Noah persists as the hero of the narrative. If we dare to identify with characters of the story other than Noah, we may be able to discern both the anthropocentric bias of the tradition and also the orientation of ecological features ignored by scholars.

In the *Adamah* Flood myth, a central figure in the text—apart from Noah and Yhwh—is *Adamah* (Gen. 6.7; 7.4, 8, 23; 8.8, 13b). The face of *Adamah* is a key idiom from earlier myths and represents not only the habitat of humanity, but also that of all fauna and flora. The fertile domain, *Adamah*, is where bio-diverse ecosystems flourish; *Adamah* is also the location of God's life-giving presence (Gen. 4.14). In the first Flood myth *Adamah* is not passive and lifeless ground whose fate and rights are insignificant: the face of *Adamah* refers to a pulsing presence that animates all ecosystems— and an impulse associated with God's presence.

In this narrative there is no indication that *Adamah* is in any way part of the problem. Rather, *Adamah* is the victim of divine actions directed against the wicked human species, *adam*. The task in this analysis is to identify with the living inhabitants of, and the habitat designated as, *Adamah*. The discussion will follow the texts of the two Flood myths included above.

2. *Species Saved from Extinction.* In the first Flood myth, the biodiversity given special attention is classified in terms of unclean and clean animals. The precise features that distinguish clean from unclean are not specified. The traditional assumption of scholars is that the distinction relates to consumption or ritual practice: any association with the unclean renders the human unclean. It is also plausible, however—given the habitat orientation of this tradition—that clean refers to those species that are viewed as clean in their environment, especially since this tradition—usually associated with the Yahwist—does not have a strong cultic thrust. Scholars argue that this distinction between clean and unclean is absent from the Priestly writer's text in the *Erets* myth because, from his perspective, the cultic law relating to this distinction has not yet been decreed by God and handed down by Moses.

The *Adamah* myth clearly focuses on animals and birds; reptiles, sea creatures or any types of flora are not considered. As the emphasis lies on preserving the seed of the species—including a 'male and his mate' as specified—Yhwh is portrayed as desiring to save all species: seven pairs of those considered clean in association with humans, and two of those who are less favored.

The preservation of these species is specified in anticipation of the impending catastrophe: the destruction of the habitat of all living things. God is about to 'blot out' or annihilate everything living on the face of *Adamah*. The habitat that sustains life, *Adamah*, will be inundated and all life will be destroyed. Previously cursed because of human sin (Gen. 3.17), *Adamah* must now experience an even greater curse because of human wickedness. Once again *Adamah*, who nurtures life, must suffer loss of life because of humans. Once again *Adamah* is the innocent party, the domain who suffers unfairly along with all her inhabitants; *Adamah* is the scapegoat!

3. *Advent of the Flood*. Noah and his entourage enter the ark in anticipation of the flood. It is ironic that in this account, the flood is explicitly caused by 40 days of rain, the very substance that is absent in primordial time and is necessary to make *Adamah* fertile (Gen. 2.5). 'Rain' is apparently a normal part of the post-Eden ecosystem of *Adamah*. In this flood narrative, rain is forced to fall for an abnormally long period of time to create a flood that renders *Adamah* uninhabitable. By this act, Yhwh upsets the natural balance of nature in the post-Eden ecosystem.

The period of rainfall is limited to 40 days and 40 nights which apparently corresponds to the duration of the flooding in this narrative. This rainfall is sufficient, however, to achieve the divine plan: to 'blot out' life on the face of *Adamah* and render *Adamah* infertile.

4. *The Ark as Habitat*. The anthropocentric orientation of this flood narrative is apparent when we consider the ark as a habitat for all life on the face of *Adamah*. There is a simplistic assumption that humans can design and manage a habitat for all creatures in a time of disaster. No consideration is given to natural factors involved in the preservation of these species. As a habitat, the ark could not provide the necessary food, living conditions and ecosystems for the many diverse forms of life: carnivores would share the same habitat as their prey; birds would share the same abode as mice.

Significantly, in Job 38–39, Yhwh makes it clear that humans like Job simply do not know the ways creatures in the wild live, feed, survive, and nurture their young. Humans are not masters over wild creatures (Job 39.9-12) and do not have a mandate to dominate them (Habel 2001). Yet, the ark is naively depicted as a single habitat where all species can live in harmony under human control.

To make the habitat scene even more problematic and claustrophobic, the ark has a covering over it. It is only when Noah removes this covering that he and all life on the ark can see the face of *Adamah*.

5. *Extent of the Flood*. In this flood narrative, the flood is clearly specified as lasting 40 days. The flood lifts the ark above *Adamah* and it floats on the water.

The description of the plight of all living creatures is poignant. The living things in the habitat of *Adamah* are described as all those creatures on the land in whose nostrils is the *neshamat-ruach chayyim* (Gen. 7.22). There is, perhaps, a hint of empathy here on the part of the narrator: this idiom might well be rendered 'the breath of the air of life'. The atmosphere that creatures on *Adamah* breathe to live is expelled and they die. To emphasize that this death by suffocation is total, the narrator also announces that Yhwh 'blots out' all life that exists on *Adamah*. In effect *Adamah* is suffocated.

6. *Termination of the Flood*. The release of a raven and doves may not be, as von Rad suggests (1961: 117), a minor unimportant detail. While it is true that ancient mariners may have released doves as compasses, the focus is not necessarily on Noah's maritime wisdom. Rather, as these birds are messengers that testify to the state of *Adamah*, their flooded habitat, they are the voice of *Adamah* communicating with Noah. For the raven there is debris upon which to float and feed. On the first mission, the dove's message regarding the state of *Adamah* is clear: I am not ready for habitation by doves. On the second mission, the dove gathers an olive branch: a message from *Adamah* that she is once again becoming a green habitat where all may inhale 'the breath of the air of life'.

The closure of the first Flood myth is a dramatic moment when Noah, cloistered inside the ark to preserve the lives of the occupants, removes the covering of the ark, looks out and beholds the landscape. Unlike most artistic versions of the ark in the flood, in this tradition Noah, his wife and family, and representative species, are battened down under a covering that protects them from the rain but also prevents them from seeing the ugly scenario outside the ark. Essentially, Noah and the ark community survive in a fabricated habitat that is completely cut off from the natural habitat where they formerly lived and flourished. The ark is tantamount to a floating refugee camp.

The liberating moment arrives, however, when Noah looks out and sees that the 'face of *Adamah*' is dry. That revelation is tantamount to an invitation from *Adamah* to return home and once again enjoy the habitat that *Adamah* provides across her face: her now dry life-giving presence. This episode may be compared with the Genesis 1 tradition where God 'beholds' part of creation and 'sees that it is good'.

b. *The Second Flood Myth*
In the second Flood myth, the text is predominantly anthropocentric with
the focus on Noah, the *adam* who does precisely as Elohim commands him;
Noah is blameless while others are corrupt—including all other creatures
(*basar*) on *Erets*. Elohim makes a covenant with Noah before the flood, but
not with the rest of creation; this only happens in Genesis 9, after the flood.
When Elohim finally remembers Noah and his entourage, Elohim ends the
flood, and the waters subside.

In this flood narrative, the key domain whose voice deserves to be heard
is *Erets*, as distinct from *Adamah* in the first flood narrative. And *Erets* is
the counterpart to *shamayim* (sky) and the habitat of all *basar* in the forms
of land, water, and mountain. *Erets*, the domain revealed on the third
day, is born from the womb of the watery deep, and stands over against
shamayim, the domain formed on the second day. Surrounded by seas after
her emergence from the deep, *Erets* is the fertile domain who cooperates
with Elohim as a partner in the six-day creation/separation process.

In the second rationale for the flood, the narrator informs us that
Erets too has become 'corrupt', not by virtue of any action on her part,
but because *Erets* has become filled with violence/lawlessness (*chamas*).
The narrator then invites us to wonder how God is going to make the
punishment fit the 'apparent crime' when God 'corrupts/destroys' *Erets* and
all *basar*. What will happen to *Erets*, the co-creator of Genesis 1? Will *Erets*
disappear forever? Will the voice of *Erets* be heard?

In the narrative that follows, our attention is drawn initially to the fate of
'all *basar*': those creatures that have 'the breath of life under *shamayim*'. It is
only with the advent of the flood that we are informed of the means whereby
Erets is to disappear and what this implies. In this narrative the event is not
a flood in the common understanding of the term and certainly far more
than the waters that resulted from 40 days and nights of rain in the first flood
narrative. In the *Erets* Flood myth the world is depicted as returning to the
primordial scenario of Gen. 1.2: *Erets* is swallowed by cosmic waters that
persist for 12 months. In this flood narrative, *Erets* is portrayed as returning
to her primordial location beneath the cosmos waters.

1. *Species Saved from Extinction*. In the second Flood myth the biodiversity
includes all animals, birds and 'creeping' creatures: all *basar*—everything
that has the breath of life. The emphasis here is not on clean and unclean,
but on ensuring that a male and female of each species is preserved to
eventually guarantee the capacity of the survivors to multiply.

As noted above, while there is a concern to preserve these species, there
is as yet no covenant with them. Elohim's covenant is with Noah who is
thereby made the agent of Elohim and who enables all *basar* to survive. A
covenant with all *basar* at this stage would have implied a personal divine

relationship with those destined to be destroyed. That personal relationship with living creatures is not established until Elohim's covenant with all *basar* after the flood. There is no explicit connection between these two covenants: one is a promise made to Noah to ensure survival; the other is a complex bond with all creation extending into the future.

2. *Advent of the Flood*. The cause of the flood in this narrative is radically different from that provided in the first narrative: instead of heavy rains, we are faced with a cosmic upheaval.

The background to this scene is the primordial world of Gen. 1.2. In this world the cosmos is a 'deep' (*tehom*) composed of waters enveloped in darkness with *Erets* residing in the deep below. After three days of creation, the deep is divided and their presence is apparent due to the advent of light. The first division locates a portion of the waters of the deep above a *raqia*, a ceiling which is called *shamayim* (sky); the second division separates another portion of the deep into what is known as 'seas'; the third division in the cosmos is caused by a geophany: the appearance of *Erets* from beneath the waters of the deep.

In this Flood myth, we are presented with a reversal of this primordial process: the 'fountains of the great deep' erupt; the waters separated to enable *Erets* to appear on day three now return to cover her completely—and *Erets* is 'buried' in the deep again.

Then the windows of heaven are opened and the celestial ocean pours down to overwhelm *Erets* and all life below. The Hebrew term '*mabbul*' does not therefore mean 'flood' in the traditional sense; it refers to the celestial or cosmic ocean which now envelops all domains (von Rad 1961: 124). This ocean is the *mabbul* on which Yhwh sits enthroned according to the ancient tradition of Psalm 29. It is this *mabbul* that overwhelms the rest of the cosmos. In the language of von Rad (1961: 124), the

> two halves of the chaotic primeval sea, separated—the one up, the other below—by God's creative government, are again united; creation begins to sink into chaos.

As noted in my analysis of Gen. 1.2, I would differ from von Rad in that I do not view the primeval sea or deep as chaos, either in the beginning or in the flood story. In my reading, the cosmic ocean is reunited and *Erets* once again resides deep within it. There is no cosmic battle or conflict with chaos; there is a return to the primordial cosmic order monitored by the *ruach* of Elohim. Instead of a wind of Elohim hovering over the waters, we now have a boat—representing life rescued from the submerged *Erets*—floating on the deep.

If, at this point, we identify with *Erets*, we find ourselves buried in the primordial deep that has the potential to be either a tomb or a womb.

We are forced to wait to discover if there is life after this 'destruction' by Elohim. We are buried deep below with *Erets* while Elohim monitors Noah and his entourage above. We are left in the dark of the deep, with no message of hope for our future.

3. *The Ark as Habitat*. The ark is constructed by Noah according to Elohim's specifications. The assumption here is that Elohim has the wisdom to provide Noah with the details necessary for a boat with three decks that will house all *basar*.

Unlike the first narrative, this version recognizes the need for this three-decker boat to store every variety of food. That presumably means grass for the herbivores, meat for the carnivores, insects and seeds for the birds and appropriate menus for the creeping and swarming creatures. If we dare to empathize with representatives of all *basar* we have a sense that the food supply indicates good intentions. The dilemma of how all this diverse hoard of living beings can cohabit for 12 months remains a mystery. As an owl dependent on mice, for example, I might find the supply and living conditions difficult!

4. *Extent of the Flood*. In the second Flood myth, the narrator seeks to emphasize the overwhelming nature of this return to the waters of a primordial cosmos. Given the open skies and the erupting deep, the narrator speaks of waters becoming 'mighty' (*gbr*), 'very mighty' and 'very, very mighty'. The might of these waters is such that they rise above 'all the mountains' under the sky. The implication is that not one portion of *Erets* is seen anywhere, no matter how high the mountains.

Finally we see how, according to this narrator, God 'destroys' *Erets* as announced earlier in Gen. 6.13: *Erets* is totally buried beneath the waters. All creatures, even 'swarming' insects, are annihilated. All creatures, even those who try to survive by climbing mountain peaks, die.

If we dare to identify with mountain goats vying for space with humans on a mountain peak, we may well have a sense that the God who created us lacks compassion. If we identify with the mountain, we may well have a sense of injustice at being unable to sustain the last vestiges of life.

5. *Termination of the Flood*. The termination of the flood is associated with Elohim 'remembering Noah' and all the creatures in the ark. 'Remembering' is often associated with a covenant as in Gen. 9.15 where the rainbow functions as reminder of Elohim's covenant after the flood. In this context, the remembering probably connects with the covenant Elohim made with Noah in Gen. 6.18.

The anthropocentric orientation of the text is highlighted by the focus on Elohim remembering Noah and his companions in the ark. At this point, Elohim does not remember *Erets*, the former co-creator, or the obliterated *Erets* community. There is no memorial for the deceased, and *Erets* is apparently a forgotten heroine.

The end of the flood is a reversal of its origins: the fountains of the deep are blocked and the windows of heaven are closed after 150 days. The landscape is given time to re-appear as on day three of creation and presumably to become fertile again. The significant addition is the wind (*ruach*) which God sends over the *Erets* to drive back the waters into the deep. In the primordial, this wind of God hovers over the waters of the deep where *Erets* lies waiting to appear (Gen. 1.2). In the flood narrative, the wind of Elohim achieves what the voice of Elohim did on day three of creation: it drives the waters back so *Erets* can appear. This scene seems to suggest a new geophany; a re-birth of *Erets*; a new beginning.

It may not be insignificant, therefore, that the dating of this re-birth falls on New Year's day in year 601 of Noah's life. The organization of the flood event according to an ancient calendar suggests stages of remembrance, the history of which has been forgotten. This calendar relates especially to *Erets*. Initially the wind of Elohim blows until the waters abate. The ark then comes to rest of a peak of *Erets* called Ararat. Finally, on New Year's day, *Erets* is declared 'dry'!

While Noah is remembered specifically, the calendar of the flood is a silent recognition of the centrality of *Erets* in the final divine plan. The initial rationale for the flood embraces a divine decision to 'corrupt/destroy *Erets*'; the calendar and termination of the flood incorporate Elohim's decision to resurrect/revive *Erets*.

The exit from the ark at Elohim's command includes a commission to breed abundantly and multiply on *Erets*. This commission recalls the blessing of Elohim in Gen. 1.22; in this context, the need to multiply abundantly is also a necessary compensation for the annihilation process that accompanied the flood.

4. *Retrieval*

In the Flood myths there are two key characters, *Adamah* and *Erets*, and their radically different accounts of the flood event can be retrieved. By identifying with these characters, rather than Noah, we can gain a new insight into the nature and orientation of these distinctive flood narratives.

The Voice of *Adamah*
I am *Adamah*, the fertile ground, the womb of mother Earth. As you may recall, I was cursed by Yhwh after Eden because of a human initiative in Eden. Outside Eden I suffered for my children and hoped, at the time, that such an unjust punishment would never happen again. But the flood was an even greater curse—and even more unjust: the flood was a cruel way of

killing all but a handful of my children with a deluge of waters that covered my entire face.

Except for Noah, his family, and representative species in a small boat, all the species I had spawned and nurtured were annihilated. Death and dead bodies were everywhere; the water curse covered my face, the entire landscape was under water. I was in great pain as one by one my children drowned in the deadly waters. Every child in whose nostrils was the breath of life suffocated.

After 40 days and nights, the heavy rains ceased, but by then my face was inundated with water and my children were dead. Noah sent out a raven from the ark; the raven found floating carcasses to ride on and eat. Then Noah sent out a dove—but this bird found no place to rest. When Noah sent out a dove the second time, I sent a message back with the dove: a tiny olive branch, to tell Noah he should leave the ark and come home.

Then came the great day: the homecoming. Noah took the canopy off of his boat and looked out across the landscape. He saw me; he beheld my face: I was dry, fertile and hospitable. Then I welcomed Noah, his family and the rest of my children home.

The Voice of *Erets*

I am *Erets*, mother Earth, the partner of Elohim in the creation of this planet. After all I did to support Elohim, I do not understand Elohim's decision to destroy me along with all the creatures I had nurtured. It was alleged that all species on the *Erets* were no longer true to their essential character. They had become abnormalities that Elohim could no longer tolerate. I, as their mother and caretaker, had to be destroyed with them. It was also alleged that my ecosystem was in chaos.

The means of destruction was a cosmic upheaval—a return to the primordial state: the windows of the sky were opened and the cosmic ocean above flooded down; the fountains of the deep were opened and the cosmic waters below erupted. The universe had returned to the primordial that existed before the seven days of creation.

And where was I? Totally enveloped in water, back in the primal womb of the deep where I rested before I was born. Alas, these waters now seemed more like a tomb than a womb.

Would I return again? Would I emerge from the primal womb and be born once again? Would Elohim remember me? Because one human was not abnormal, but righteous, Elohim decided to rescue one family of humans and pairs of each species on a boat called an ark. In this ark they survived a flood that lasted more than 12 months.

Finally Elohim remembered Noah and the inhabitants of the ark. I like to think Elohim also remembered me.

Anyway, Elohim sent the wind that used to hover over the primordial waters of the deep in the very beginning to blow back the waters that covered me. It was the wind of Elohim—rather than the voice of Elohim—that led to my re-appearance, my second birth. One signal that this was also a birth, a new beginning, is the date given for my first appearance: the first day of the first month of the 601st year of Noah's life.

When Noah and the animals emerged, my landscape was dry and all the species were encouraged by Elohim to be fruitful and multiply, the assumption being that I would provide food and shelter for all species as I had before the flood, The pain of my interim destruction was replaced with a sense of purpose: I was again home and mother for all my children.

Chapter 9

GENESIS 8.20–9.29:
POST-FLOOD CHANGES IN *ADAMAH* AND *ERETS*

1. *Design*

The Flood myths represent the flood event as a massive catastrophe resulting in the destruction of Earth and life on Earth. According to the first narrator, humans are not behaving as God intended prior to the flood. According to the second narrator, the same is true for all living species. A key question arises: Will God change components of creation after the catastrophe or leave them as they were pre-flood? Other questions follow:

- Will *Adamah* retain the pre-flood curse?
- Will *Erets* relate to God in the same way as pre-flood?
- Will the animal world experience any significant changes?
- Will humans be viewed as they were pre-flood?

A series of traditions are cited in response to these and related questions. The organization of these responses does not suggest a particular literary design or narrative pattern. Rather, the answers are presented as a series of divine responses without any obvious connecting features between them.

Understandably, these reference the two rationales for the flood given in Genesis 6 and the conditions prevailing prior to the flood. The dilemma faced by the Creator: will these conditions persist, and if so, what needs to change. And the ultimate question: is the flood a failure and, if so, how will God come to terms with the consequences?

Consistent with the terminology of the two rationales in the flood narratives, *Adamah* and *Erets* persist as key characters in the post-flood narratives: in the first flood narrative, Yhwh's relationship to Noah, humanity, living creatures and *Adamah* is radically changed; in the second, God's relationship with Noah, humanity, living creatures and *Erets* is re-defined in terms of covenant promises. A radical change in divine attitude is reflected in both the *Adamah* and *Erets* myths, and indicates a new relationship between God and nature that may well be designated green. The greening dimension is summarized later in this chapter.

Some scholars, like Frymer-Kensky (1988: 67), claim that, given the post-flood situation, God's first act is to give humans laws to control their behaviour. However, God gives humans only one law: a law against the shedding of blood. The other elements of the narrative seek to answer the question of how God will change creation post-flood. After all, the flood is a failure.

> The *Adamah* Myth: Genesis 8.20-22
>> Changes to *Adamah* and to the Seasons
>> Response of Noah: animal sacrifices
>> Initial Response of Yhwh: enjoys the aroma
>> First Divine Change: curses removed from *Adamah*
>> Second Divine Change: all creatures never again destroyed
>> Third Divine Change: Earth to enjoy regular seasons
>
> The *Tselem* Myth: Genesis 9.1-7
>> Changes to Animal–Human Life
>> The Blessing of Fertility: humans to fill *Erets*
>> First Divine Change: animals invested with fear
>> Second Divine Change: humans turned into carnivores
>> Third Divine Change: drinking blood forbidden
>> Fourth Divine Change: the *tselem* of Elohim reinforced
>
> The *Erets* Myth: Genesis 9.8-17
>> Changes to *Erets* and Life on *Erets*:
>> Covenant Announced: all in the ark included
>> First Divine Change: no flood to again destroy life or *Erets*
>> Second Divine Change: rainbow a sign of covenant with *Erets*
>> Third Divine Change: Elohim will remember the covenant
>
> Changes to Human Society: Genesis 9.18-19

2. Analysis

a. The Adamah Myth—Changes to Adamah and the Seasons (Genesis 8.20-22)

1. *Genesis 8.20: The Response of Noah.* The response of Noah is perhaps understandable in terms of modes of thanksgiving found in the ancient world. However, in the context of the massive slaughter of living creatures in the flood and the principle of preserving species by means of the ark, the killing of a representative of every species of clean bird and animal that survived in the ark seems inconsistent and downright foolish.

If we now dare to identify with these sacrificed living kin, we realize that they have been companions with Noah throughout the flood. In that context, they presumably have a sense of gratitude that they have survived. But Noah is willing to kill these innocent survivors just as Yhwh has killed all their families in the flood. Noah is portrayed as insensitive to the plight of those who died and the hopes of those who survived. Pleasing Yhwh now seems to be far more important than preserving life.

2. *Genesis 8.21: Yhwh's First Change.* Significantly, Yhwh does not censure Noah for killing a myriad of precious survivors on an altar, but like an indulgent master relishes the sensuous aroma of this massive holocaust of burning creatures. This aroma leads Yhwh, according to this narrator, to start talking to himself. Finally, after numerous acts of divine judgment and destruction, we meet a deity who is willing to re-assess the situation, reverse past actions, and change creation.

The reason Yhwh gives for this reversal, however, is not that Yhwh is genuinely sorry for the cruel treatment of humanity and all life on *Adamah*, but rather, that the flood has not rectified the problem facing Yhwh before the flood: the sinful impulses of the human heart. Yhwh openly admits that the condition of human sinfulness persists after the flood. If the flood is intended as a shock tactic to bring humans to contrition, it obviously fails.

In other words, the flood is a failure! The judgment of destruction imposed on all living creatures does not overcome the problem of human sinfulness. The rest of humanity and their kin in creation apparently die in vain, and now Yhwh has to come to terms with the outcome of this tragic situation. The God who is said to be 'sorry' for having created humans prior to the flood must now come to terms with his guilt and gruesome actions.

Anthropocentric readings, such as that of von Rad, view Yhwh's response to the sacrifice as the sign of a new relationship between Yhwh and humanity; the sacrifice is interpreted as an indication of human confession and a perceived need for reconciliation (von Rad 1961: 118). A close reading, however, indicates no confession of sinfulness by Noah and his family, or any desire for reconciliation. Yhwh faces the continued sinfulness of humanity and takes a necessary step to help combat the problem.

The divine reversal is striking! 'I will never again curse *Adamah* because of *adam*!' The change is bold and liberating.

This remarkable reversal takes us back to Yhwh's very first act of judgment after Eden when Yhwh declares to the primal pair: 'cursed is *Adamah* because of you (*adam*)'. The flood, like the curse pronounced on *Adamah* after Eden, is a punishment imposed on the fertile domains of nature—not because of their misdeeds, but because of human sin. Now, with the revoking of this curse, nature will no longer suffer divine curses because of human sinfulness. Mother Nature will no longer need to suffer vicariously for her children. The natural order is declared safe from divine acts of judgment provoked by human deeds. At least, that seems to be the intent of the change.

The reversal in this Flood myth is not simply that Yhwh accepts humans an inherently sinful, but that *Adamah* is now the focus of divine attention. The primordial curse, which in mythic terms has been viewed as identifying a fixed component of the cosmos, is now reversed: *Adamah* in no longer cursed. Creation has been restored. Nature is free from any such curse. Yhwh has liberated *Adamah*, in spite of the addiction of humans to sin.

3. Genesis 8.22: Yhwh's Second Change. Yhwh's promise to liberate nature is further explicated in the closing edict which incorporates an additional promise:

> As long as *Erets* endures,
> seed time and harvest,
> cold and heat,
> summer and winter,
> day and night,
> shall not cease (Gen. 8.22).

Without the curse on *Adamah* the seasonal patterns of the natural order—by which *adam* will labour to obtain food and sustenance—is guaranteed. In contemporary language, Yhwh guarantees there will be no climate change. The weather patterns that accompany a stable agrarian lifestyle will be maintained. There is no longer any divine curse on the ecosystems of climate and the weather.

If we dare to identify now with *Adamah*, we experience an extraordinary sense of relief. Instead of being vulnerable to disastrous divine interventions because of Yhwh's attitude to humans, the fertile landscape of *Adamah* is free to nurture her progeny in a consistent cycle of climate, weather patterns and seasons. Finally, *Adamah* seems to have been treated fairly by her landlord.

b. *The* Tselem *Myth—Changes to Animal–Human Life (Genesis 9.1-7)*

1. Genesis 9.1-7: The Blessing of Fertility. The second set of changes reported by the narrator commences with a blessing of fertility on Noah and his progeny. They are to multiply and fill *Erets*. The blessing imparted to the first humans is re-instated. Here there is apparently no change: the violent tragedy of the flood has not brought procreation to an end, even if all but a few humans survived. Noah is the new *adam*.

In the original blessing (Gen. 1.28), the purpose given for filling *Erets* is to subdue it and bring it under human control. The omission of the term 'subdue' here may suggest that humans are no longer expected to dominate *Erets* as before; however, it is very clear from the verses that follow that humans will dominate the animal world. The blessing of fertility is repeated at the close of this unit to emphasize, it would seem, that procreation is pivotal to the future of humankind. After all, only Noah and his family survive and they need to multiply immediately.

2. Genesis 9.2: Elohim's First Change. The previous verse verified that human fertility will continue throughout *Erets*. Will *adam* still be expected to 'dominate' the animal world as announced in the original blessing of Gen.1.28? It appears so, but there are several differences.

First, by announcing that all living things are 'delivered/given into your hand', Elohim clearly gives humans the power and authority to dominate the world of living creatures, whether they inhabit water, land or air. The sovereignty of humans persists, in spite of the fact that the animal world suffers unjustly in the flood. The big difference, however, is that Elohim invests all living creatures with a 'fear and dread' of humans—a condition resulting in total domination (cf. Deut. 11.25).

Humans are now transformed into beings that terrify the rest of the animal world. Where is the justice in this? Clearly, this tradition reflects an extreme reversal of the peaceful memory of Eden and the prophetic dream of lions, lambs and humans dwelling in harmony. It also suggests a perception of pre-flood life as idyllic, even though the rationales for the flood depict a world of sin and lawlessness.

From the perspective of our kin in all domains of creation, this heightening of the mandate to dominate is frightening and unwelcome. Humans and all living creatures suffered the same cruel fate in the flood. Did they all die in vain? We might well expect a new world order after the flood where humans are given a mandate to preserve their kin. After all, doesn't the ark symbolize the preservation of all species? Alas, the post-flood changes introduce the harsh reality of the human desire for domination.

3. *Genesis 9.3: Elohim's Second Change.* Consistent with the first divine change, humans are now given the right to kill all creatures except humans. Fauna may now be treated in the same way as flora and killed by humans for food. The text reports that humans are 'given' everything. On the surface that may mean everything from ants to elephants, but the context suggests that the beings concerned are those appropriate to eat. In any case, Elohim has changed humans from herbivores into carnivores and thereby intensified their domination over nature.

4. *Genesis 9.4: Elohim's Third Change.* To this point in the textual traditions, living creatures are identified as 'Earth-made', that is, made from *Adamah*, and variously identified as *nephesh chayyah* (living being), *adam* (Earth being), *'aphar* (dust) and *basar* (flesh). Living creatures are animated with the *nishmat chayyim* (breath of life) or *ruach chayyim* (wind of life) which comes directly from God. Now a new dimension of living beings is revealed as sacred: their *dam* (blood). Blood is identified specifically as the *nephesh* (life) of the creature.

While humans are now transformed into carnivores, they are not permitted to drink blood, which is the life given to a living being from God. The life of the creature belongs to God; only the flesh is available for humans to consume. In the later cultic laws of Israel, anyone who dares to drink blood is to be severed from their kin (Lev. 7.26ff.), and poured out like water (Deut. 12.16). The mandate in Genesis, however, is not cultic in nature; it is revealed as a universal change announced for all life after the flood. Ultimately every *nephesh* belongs to God (Ezek. 18.4).

Significantly, while humans have the same essential characteristics as other Earth beings with flesh, breath and blood, they are privileged creatures: they, unlike other living beings, have the right to kill their non-human kin for food. From the perspective of other Earth beings, the special treatment of humans after the flood seems unjustified and preferential.

5. *Genesis 9.5-6: Elohim's Fourth Change.* The fourth change relates to the sanctity of life—more specifically, of human life. While humans are free to kill animals, they are not free to kill each other. Animals are likewise forbidden to kill humans. Elohim requires reckoning for any killing of a human: whoever kills *adam* is to be killed.

The basis for this mandate is twofold: the killer is spilling the blood of another—blood that has been given by God to animate that being. The second ground is that all humans are made in the *tselem* of Elohim.

Given the description of how humans behaved prior to the flood, it might be inferred that they no longer bear the *tselem* of Elohim. Certainly their moral and spiritual behaviour is totally ungodlike! However, as this Genesis 9 text reveals, they do retain Elohim's *tselem*.

The language of this passage seems to support the argument adduced earlier: the *tselem* of Elohim refers to the living human being as a being of flesh, breath and now blood who can be physically killed; the *tselem* is not connected to some inner dimension, such as reason, consciousness or soul. Just as a bull may serve as a visible image of the god Baal, humans possess the *tselem* of Elohim and represent God by exercizing power over living creatures and *Erets*. To kill one such human is to smash a living *tselem* residing on *Erets*.

If we identify with *Erets*, we may sense something of the horror of the flood event. As a consequence of being destroyed by a flood, *Erets* becomes the graveyard for an entire population of living beings bearing the *tselem* of Elohim. She witnesses Elohim destroying numerous beings who bear this *tselem*. The sight is almost impossible to imagine, but ultimately the blood of these living beings cries out from *Erets* just as Abel's blood cried out from *Adamah*.

Taken as whole, Gen. 9.1-7 represents a revised version of the *Tselem* myth found in Gen. 1.26-28. This new version might be summarized as follows:

> Let me re-make humans in my *tselem*,
> In the *tselem* of Elohim, in my likeness.
> Let me make them flesh and blood
> And let them multiply to fill *Erets*.
> Let them rule all living creatures,
> Who will be terrified of humans
> Because I have given them into human hands.
> Let them kill living beings for food

But not drink their life blood.
Let them not kill each other
Or shed each other's blood
For they are my living representatives,
Walking and ruling *Erets* in my stead.

c. *The* Erets *Myth—Changes to* Erets *and Life on* Erets *(Genesis 9.8-17)*
The third major domain where God chooses to change conditions and
relationships after the flood pertains to *Erets* and life on *Erets*. This particular
text has evoked considerable response in recent times since it announces a
positive portrait of the Creator's bond with creation. Before analysing this
significant bond and its implications, we need to keep in mind the pre-flood
context and the implied change of divine attitude to life on *Erets*.

According to the second pre-flood rationale (Gen. 6.11-13), *Erets* is
declared 'corrupt' or 'spoiled' (*shachat*) because she is filled with 'violence'
or 'lawlessness' (*chamas*). Creation has become 'spoiled' in God's eyes. Why?
Because all *basar* has corrupted their 'ways' on *Erets*! The natural order of
things has broken down and living creatures are not living according to
their inner character. This condition provokes Elohim to 'destroy' (*shachat*)
all flesh and *Erets* as well.

How have conditions changed after the flood? Are living creatures
now true to their nature? Is *Erets* no longer polluted? Nothing in the text
suggests that these domains are transformed or changed. What changes, it
seems, is the orientation of Elohim.

1. *Genesis 9.8-10: Elohim Makes a Covenant with all* Basar. After the flood,
Elohim chooses to reorient divine relationships with 'all *basar*' and 'all
living creatures' including humans. As John Olley has demonstrated, the
repeated use of these two expressions in this text illustrates that God's
special new relationship with nature embraces all life, not only human life
(2000: 136). The negative verdict on 'all flesh' in the pre-flood rationale is
superseded.

This new relationship is declared to be a 'covenant' (*berit*). Throughout
the Hebrew Scriptures a covenant implies that two parties participate
in the bond that is established, whether or not the parties are equal or
formally agree to that bond. All *basar* now has a personal relationship with
Elohim. Elohim is now committed to maintaining this personal relationship
with all *basar*. In Gen. 9.8-10, human and non-human domains are not
differentiated; both enjoy the same covenant bond with Elohim.

2. *Genesis 9.11: First Divine Change—No Flood to Destroy Life or* Erets. The
first change that happens after the flood according to this narrator is that,
because of the new covenant relationship Elohim has with all *basar*, a flood
will never again destroy all flesh or *Erets*. Elohim's new relationship with
all *basar* means they and *Erets* are now valued in a way that did not exist

before the flood. Destruction of creation is no longer an option for Elohim within this covenant.

It is significant that *Erets* is now included in this divine edict. The fate of *Erets* and all *basar* is linked just as they were before the flood. Though Elohim devalues *Erets* by allowing humans to 'subdue' her, through this new covenant *Erets* is given a positive status.

3. *Genesis 9.12-13: Second Divine Change—Rainbow as a Sign of Covenant with* Erets. Evidence of the change of divine attitude and the corresponding covenant bond with all living beings is the rainbow which Elohim creates specifically for this agreement. While we might assume that the rainbow previously existed within the weather patterns of *Erets*, this new creation demonstrates that the flood story is also a primordial origin myth that relates how various dimensions of the cosmos come into being.

The striking development associated with the advent of the rainbow is the announcement that this covenant is extended: Elohim not only establishes a covenant with humans and all *basar*, but also with *Erets*. According to the second rationale for the flood, *Erets* is 'corrupt' and filled with lawlessness, because the 'way' of all flesh is 'corrupt'. As a result Elohim decides to 'corrupt/destroy' *Erets* along with all *basar*.

In effect, the flood 'destroys' *Erets*, drowning her beneath cosmic waters. When the waters are blown back, *Erets* re-appears as on day three of creation. God apparently now relates to *Erets* in a new way: this new relationship is a personal covenant with *Erets*.

The designation of the rainbow as a sign parallels other covenants where domains of nature are cited as witnesses to a covenant agreement between two parties. In Josh. 24.27 a stone hears the words of the covenant and acts as a witness. In the case of a broken covenant in Mic. 6.1-2, the mountains, the hills and the very foundations of *Erets* are summoned as witnesses before the court. In Genesis 9 the rainbow witnesses the covenant.

4. *Genesis 9.14-17: Third Divine Change—Elohim Remembers the Covenant.* The rainbow, however, also serves as a constant reminder to God of the new relationship that now exists between God, all flesh and *Erets*—with special emphasis on the promise never to destroy all *basar* on *Erets*.

At this point it is appropriate to refer to an article by an Indigenous Australian, Wally Fejo. From his perspective, God, the Rainbow Spirit, is not outside *Erets*, but deep within her, so when *Erets* is corrupted by human evils, she needs to be cleansed by God.

> When the Earth is concealed by water, the situation returns to the way it was in the beginning of the Dreaming (Gen. 1.2). The Earth is beneath the waters again. God is beneath the waters again. God is not at some distance watching the flood with an expression of justified anger. God experiences the flood, the death of life on Earth (2000: 142).

Whether or not the narrator of Genesis 9 viewed the Creator as immanent in *Erets* may be debated. The insights of Fejo, however, make us aware that there is a spiritual relationship between Elohim, *Erets*, and the rainbow. The rainbow is not only a living expression of Elohim's promise to *Erets*, but also a living expression of Elohim's presence connected with *Erets*. While the text may not quite reflect the perspective of Fejo that 'the rainbow is a revelation of the Rainbow Spirit (God)' (2000: 145), it nevertheless indicates that the rainbow is a spiritual connection between God and *Erets*.

The establishment of the rainbow covenant can therefore be recognized as a significant change in the way Elohim relates to *Erets* and all *basar* that inhabit *Erets*.

5. *The Greening Dimension.* In the context of the current environmental crisis and the cruel treatment of nature in the two preceding catastrophe myths, we may well ask whether there are any significant indications of a greening process in the wake of the flood. Does the God of either myth finally move from grey actions to green actions? Here I shall summarize briefly some of the findings given above that may be identified as the greening dimension of the post-flood changes.

In the *Adamah* myth two vital decisions of Yhwh enable a full restoration of nature, and the greening of *Adamah*. The first decision involves the bold removal of the curse imposed on *Adamah* because of human sin. Now, in spite of the persistence of sinful human impulses, *Adamah* is free from the curse.

The removal of the curse means that nature is fully alive once again, fully green and vibrant. Now there is no fallen creation, no dark side to nature because of human sin. Nature is free of the curse, liberated to become lush, green and plentiful. In other words, in this tradition, the divine policy of injuring creation because of humans—operative since Eden—has been reversed.

The second greening action of Yhwh is the divine guarantee that the cycles of nature will not be interrupted. Given this guarantee, greening is assured; seed-time and harvest will persist—whether for humans, birds, or animals. Seed-time guarantees green-time; cold and heat guarantees seasons, including winter and summer, rest and growth. Night and day guarantee the cycle of light that generates greenness in nature.

The *Adamah* myth does not simply end with the cessation of the flood as such. Rather, this myth has Yhwh initiating a positive greening process in nature that reverses destructive actions associated with the flood. The Flood myth in this tradition is far from green, but the culmination of the narrative identifies Yhwh, who is initially 'sorry' for creating humans (Gen. 6.6) and ready to destroy all life, as committed now to sustaining nature.

The greening dimension of the *Erets* myth is also dramatic. We recall that the birth of Earth (Gen. 1.9-13) is explicitly associated with greening.

Not only does *Erets* emerge from the womb of the primordial deep at the instigation of Elohim; *Erets* also becomes green, alive with all forms of flora—vegetation that *Erets* produces from within herself. Green would appear to be the evidence for Elohim that baby *Erets* is alive.

The crucial green action of Elohim in this catastrophe myth is the covenant that Elohim makes with *Erets*. In spite of the extended destruction of all forms of life because *Erets* has become full of violence, all flesh has corrupted its way, and creation has been spoiled, *Erets* is ready to begin again. When the primordial deep recedes on new year's day, *Erets* is again visible. *Erets* is born again to become green once again. Elohim is now ready to restore life on *Erets* and initiate a new nurturing relationship with *Erets*: a covenant relationship.

The promise of continued life on *Erets*, with no more eruptions of the deep or opening of the skies to flood *Erets*, is more than a passing phase. The promise of Elohim is a covenant: a personal bond between Elohim and nature. Elohim promises that *Erets* will never lose her vitality because of a flood. Elohim's covenant loyalty is a guarantee that *Erets* will be green forever.

The *Tselem* myth (Gen. 9.1-7), embedded between these two greening traditions, reflects no greening dimension; rather, it interrupts the greening actions of Elohim—much as this myth interrupts the creation process in Gen. 1.26-28. In spite of the grey orientation of the *tselem* tradition, both the *Erets* myth and the *Adamah* myth reflect a radical reversal of the divine attitude to nature. From now on, everything—from the seasons to the soil—will be part of a brand new green world with a rainbow to keep God honest.

d. *Changes to Human Society (Genesis 9.18-29)*

1. *Genesis 9.18-23: Noah's Celebrations.* The final post-flood narrative is a separate legend associated with Noah whose progeny are said to have peopled the whole Earth. Noah, however, is described—like Cain—as a man of *Adamah*: an agriculturalist.

Noah plants a vineyard, makes wine, gets drunk and lies naked in his tent. Ham sees his father's nakedness and goes outside to tell his two brothers. Shem and Japheth then take a garment and walk backwards, turning their faces away, so that they do not also see their father's nakedness.

The vine is a noble symbol of joy for humankind, a gift for celebrating life (Ps. 104.15; Gen. 49.11ff.; Mic. 4.4). If this tradition is consistent with the *Adamah* Flood myth, Noah's celebration with vines and wine reflects the possibility of *adam* now enjoying the removal of the curse from *Adamah* (Gen. 8.21).

However, celebration turns into shame. While the text emphasizes that the two brothers are only concerned about covering their father's nakedness, there is a possible innuendo that Ham may have done more than 'see' his father's nakedness. When Ruth, for example, uncovers the feet of Boaz, the sexual implications are obvious. A similar implication may also be discerned here.

2. Genesis 9.24-27: The Cursing of Canaan, the Progeny of Ham. Whatever the immodesty of Ham may have been, it is Canaan who experiences the anger and consequently the curse of Ham. This curse announces a change in human society—the advent of slavery. Canaan is to become the slave of his brothers Shem and Japheth, a condition that will be perpetuated in subsequent generations. Canaan is cursed for whatever his father may have done.

This text probably reflects a popular aetiology about the sexual depravity of the Canaanites that is used to justify the Israelite conquest of the land (Lev. 18.24). That Yhwh should sanction such a curse seems totally unwarranted. If we identify with Canaan, the land and the people, we can recognize a racial bias that deserves to be exposed. As we will see in the next chapter, there are also traditions about Canaan that are positive and recognize the land of Canaan as a place of hospitality and goodwill, not depravity and degradation. That Canaanites are destined to be the slaves of the children of Shem from the days of the flood, because of what Ham does, seems totally unjust.

To add insult to injury, vineyards and olive trees flourish in Canaan. When the Israelites enter the land they take over vines they did not plant (Deut. 6.10-11). The curse of Canaan extends, it seems, to the aggressive occupation of the landscape by the Israelites.

2. Retrieval

The Voice of *Adamah*

What an amazing turn-around! What an extraordinary about-face! Yhwh finally came to his senses! After imposing one curse after another on me because of the way humans acted, after making me the scapegoat for human sin for generations, after punishing the innocent along with the guilty, Yhwh finally faced facts: humans sin willy nilly! And Yhwh's punishments on me were unfair!

So Yhwh removed the curse I had endured since Eden. Suddenly I was free, free to nurture, flourish, blossom and grow as I once did in Eden. Amazing! All my ecosystems would be allowed to function naturally again.

In addition, there would be no barriers to my evolution as a fertile landscape, no weather patterns or seasonal changes, no catastrophes or climate changes to hinder my growth. I was now free to be myself, Mother Nature, glorious and green.

The Voice of the Animals

Things have gone from bad to worse. Before the flood, we were told that humans represented God and that we, Earth beings like humans, were to be dominated by humans. Before the flood, all life on Earth became chaotic and God sent a flood that destroyed us. We seemed to have no value in God's eyes. We were murdered by the cosmic flood waters—without any compassion from above.

After the flood, we were told that humans still have control, they still represented God and that now it was perfectly acceptable for humans to kill animals for food. We in turn were not permitted to kill humans. Why? Because we share the same life blood as humans!

We are Earth beings like humans. Why should we be treated as lesser beings, delivered into the hands of humans like slaves?

The Voice of *Erets*

What a great change in Elohim. Before the flood Elohim denounced all living creatures as corrupt, not living in tune with their inner nature. Now after the flood Elohim was ready, not only to accept living creatures as they are, but also to enter into a personal covenant with them, promising never to destroy them again.

Elohim even made a covenant with me after earlier threatening to destroy me in cosmic waters. Elohim bonded with me as a partner in nature. God even created a rainbow to testify to this new agreement. Whenever I display a rainbow, Elohim will remember me, my living creatures and the covenant with Elohim.

It is great to see the change in Elohim. I hope it continues.

The Voice of Canaan

After the flood my grandfather enjoyed his work in the fields, growing vineyards and celebrating with the wines he grew. On one occasion he got a little drunk and lay naked in his tent. My father Ham saw him lying naked and told the brothers; they came and covered him.

I don't know just why, but when my grandfather awoke he let out a string of curses against me. He declared that I was to be the lowest of slaves beneath my uncles.

How unfair! How biased and cruel!

Generations later, when the children of Shem came into my land, the land of Canaan, they took all the lands I had nurtured with olives and vineyards. They came and drank my wine. But they never toasted me.

How unfair! How biased and cruel!

Chapter 10

GENESIS 10.1–11.32:
ERETS AFTER THE FLOOD

1. *Design*

The sheer volume of the text of Genesis 10 and 11 dedicated to human genealogies easily directs our attention away from the presence of Earth and the domains of Earth that are crucial to the import of these chapters. The geographical and cultural dimensions of this text, however, are just as significant as the genealogical.

Cassuto, for example, maintains that the purpose of Genesis 10 is to show how the whole Earth was peopled from the three sons of Noah. Genesis 11, he argues, constitutes a completion and sequel of the history of the sons of Noah identified in Genesis 10 (1964: 172, 225). Like most scholars, Cassuto focuses primarily on the sons of Noah, but pays little attention to the flood as the immediate context and Earth as the domain being peopled; however, Genesis 10–11 is ultimately also concerned with Earth as well as human beings on Earth and their relationship with Earth.

The expression 'after the flood' is a pivotal term that frames Genesis 10 (Gen. 10.1, 32), and links this chapter with the preceding flood narrative and with the Noah tradition (Gen. 9.28). This pivotal expression anticipates the alternative account of what happens after the flood (Gen. 11.1) and links with two *toledoth* references that are part of the wider framing of the latter chapters of Genesis 1–11.

'After the flood', however, is more than a connecting narrative idiom. This expression identifies the condition and context of Earth as a key figure. According to the *Erets* myth, Elohim 'destroys' *Erets* and all the inhabitants—except for Noah and his boatload of creatures (Gen. 6.13). When *Erets* is inundated and all life—fauna and flora—are submerged, *Erets* is 'destroyed' by Elohim and devalued in the process. 'After the flood' also means 'after the destruction' of *Erets* by God.

After the flood, the initial scene is clearly one of total devastation: the ugly remains of the catastrophe are scattered across the landscape. After the flood, Earth must again bring forth life. After the flood, there needs to be a new beginning, comparable to the first. Earth must come to life again, in spite of how God has treated her in the flood. The covenant of God never to repeat the flood may well be the impetus for Earth to be born again. Is there genuine hope for Earth after the flood—or rather, is there genuine hope that *Erets* can repair what God has done to Earth and the Earth community in the flood?

There are two accounts of how life spreads across this devastated domain called 'Earth'. The first describes a natural migration of people who are born, settle, create cultures and become nations across Earth (Genesis 10). Earth is the habitat that enables this new beginning. In the second account, Yhwh is an agent intervening directly in the process of human dispersion across Earth; this story focuses on the potential of one chosen family (Genesis 11).

Bernhard Anderson views the second account, the Tower of Babel story, as 'the climax of the primeval history whose meaning and scope are universal' (1994: 167). He also recognizes the primordial diversity of culture expressed in the legends of Genesis 10. He points out that theologians of the Middles Ages viewed sin, exemplified at Babel, as the cause of diversity in the cultural communities. Most scholars still ignore the implications of the alternative tradition in Genesis 10.

A Structural Analysis of the Diverse Traditions of Genesis 10–11

Genesis 10: *Erets* after the Flood—Human Migration
    Framing Superscription (Genesis 10.1)
        the *toledoth* of Noah post-flood
    Migration Legends
        The Legend of Japheth (Genesis 10.2-5)
            genealogy, geography and cultures
        The Legend of Ham (Genesis 10.6-14)
            genealogy, geography and cultures
        The Legend of Canaan (Genesis 10.15-20)
            genealogy, geography and cultures
        The Legend of Shem (Genesis 10.21-31)
            genealogy, geography and cultures
    Framing Summation (Genesis 10.32)
        the migration of *toledoth* across Earth post-flood
Chapter 11.1-9: *Erets* after the Flood—Divine Intervention
    Tower of Babel Myth (Genesis 11.1-9)
Chapter 11.10-32: *Erets* after the Flood—Human Migration
    Framing Superscription (Genesis 11.10)
        the *toledoth* of Shem (Gen. 11.10-26)
    Migration Legend
        The Legend of Terah (Genesis 11.27-32)
            genealogy, family and migration

In Genesis 10–11 we have a cluster of legends whose initial setting is 'after the flood'. While an initial reading may give the impression that the focus is entirely on family histories, a close reading reveals that geography and genealogy are both integral to the development of cultures. Earth and the domains of Earth play a key role in the context and plot of these legends. Our task is to read as Earth beings and to discern the role and voice of Earth in the transformation of peoples after the flood.

a. *The Tower of Babel Myth*
A detailed analysis of the literary structure of the Tower of Babel myth reveals a subtle narrative involving Earth, humans and Yhwh, a story replete with irony and suspense, described as 'a masterpiece of narrative art' (Anderson 1994: 168), and as an inspired rhetorical narrative (Kikawada 1975). Anderson's analysis of the narrative design, however, ignores the role of Earth. He reads the narrative strictly as an interaction between humans and the divine, as is apparent in his plan of the narrative.

> Introduction: the original situation (Gen. 11.1)
>   Human action
>   a.   narrative report (Gen. 11.2): wanderers settle on the plain
>   b.   discourse with twofold invitational exclamations (Gen. 11.3-4)
>   Divine action
>   a.   narrative report (Gen. 11.5): investigation of the building
>   b.   divine discourse with twofold invitational exclamations
>   (Gen. 11.6, 7)
>   c.   narrative report of divine action (Gen. 11.9): dispersion
> Conclusion: return to the beginning but on a new level of meaning
>   (Gen. 11.9)

Earth is clearly the point of departure for the plot and the location after resolution of the plot. While humans are the dominant characters, their relationship with Earth is crucial in terms of origin, plot, and outcome. I would therefore outline the narrative structure of this myth as follows:

> Setting: humans gathering from all of Earth (Gen. 11.1-2)
>   common language on Earth
>   central location on Earth
> Catalyst: humans reaching for the skies (Gen. 11.3-4)
>   impetus: desire to build
>   motive: fear of dispersion
> Response: divine Intervention (Gen. 11.5-8)
>   descent by Yhwh
>   analysis by Yhwh
>   decision by Yhwh
> Closure: dispersion of humans into all of Earth (Gen. 11.9)

2. Analysis

a. Introduction

Terra nullius is the official term used to designate territories or lands that have no inhabitants or, more precisely, have no legal human inhabitants. This spurious designation was employed by powers such as the British Empire in the nineteenth century to justify the invasion and conquest of lands such as Australia and in the twentieth century to justify the Jewish settlement of Palestine. The indigenous inhabitants and their cultures are viewed as legally non-existent. The non-human inhabitants are viewed as legitimate prey. In line with the mandate to dominate in Gen. 1.26-28, the invaders believe they have a divine right to conquer peoples and harness nature.

It might be argued that the accounts of Genesis 10–11 assume a genuine *terra nullius* orientation as their point of departure. After all, the flood apparently annihilated all peoples and living creatures from the face of Earth. 'After the flood' implies a world in which the skeletons of past families and creatures adorn the landscape. The face of Earth reflects the face of death. If, as a reader, I dare to identify with Earth in this context, I experience a sense of utter desolation and abuse. I am inundated by debris and death.

The text of Genesis 10, however, does not dwell on the condition of Earth but looks forward to new generations of families emerging in time. The idiom 'after the flood' also recalls day three of creation (Genesis 1) when Earth emerges from the primordial waters as a primal *terra nullius*. 'After the flood' also means a new beginning for a devastated Earth just as it does for a destroyed humanity. 'After the flood' suggests the re-birth of Earth as the waters disperse.

Cassuto maintains that the intent of Genesis 10 is not geological. Rather he holds that the purpose is (a) to show that Divine Providence is reflected in the distribution of the nations over the face of Earth no less than in other acts of the world's creation and administration; (b) to determine relationship between the peoples of Israel and the other peoples; (c) to teach the unity of post-diluvian humanity, which, like ante-diluvian humanity, is wholly descended from one pair of beings (1964: 175).

Significantly, God is not mentioned as a character in Genesis 10, though the wider context implies a divine providence or primal blessing that some scholars discern in the text. Nor is Israel identified. If, however, we recognize the presence of Earth and the domains of Earth—after the flood—we may revise Cassuto's articulation of the purpose of the Genesis 10 as follows: (a) to show how Earth, after the disaster of the flood, provides a home for humans who provoked the flood; (b) to identify the geography that provides habitats for the diverse cultures associated with the peoples of Earth; (c) to recognize the natural interconnection between spreading humanity and the domains of Earth.

The dispersal of humanity and the habitation of domains on Earth are treated as a natural progression with no specific intervention by God. Lands are identified and languages created during the course of time. In Genesis 10, God is not introduced as a character directing the course of natural or human history after the flood. In contrast to the Tower of Babel myth (Genesis 11), in Genesis 10 God retires into the background.

b. *Framing Superscription (Genesis 10.1): Noah's Post-Flood* Toledoth
As noted above, the expression 'after the flood' identifies the world of the narrative. The horrendous events of the flood itself, the universal devastation, and the subsequent repentance by God all remain in the background. The narrator initially focuses, in rather anthropocentric and androcentric fashion, only on the four male humans who survive. The women and the animals are ignored; Earth and Earth's domains are yet to be identified. The story it seems is about the mastery of the hero, Noah. He survives and his family multiplies.

The announcement of the post-flood *toledoth* of Noah indicates that this superscription is part of the framing of Genesis 1–11 and provides an introduction to the genealogical and geological legends that follow.

c. *Genesis 10.2-5: The Legend of Japheth*
The legend of Japheth consists of a genealogy (Gen. 10.2-4) and a summary statement of locations, languages and peoples (Gen. 10.5).

Numerous scholars have explored the identities of the various 'sons' of Japheth. Some of these names refer to peoples mentioned elsewhere in the Bible, people such as Magog (Ezek. 38.2) or Tubal and Meshech (Ezek. 27.13). In general, scholars have suggested that these peoples who descended from Japheth seem to be located to the north of Israel.

Especially significant are the geographical and social dimensions of the legend. The progeny of Japeth are the source of peoples who spread to islands and are dispersed along the coast. These particular habitats are integral to the development of their cultures, including languages and social structures. This natural dispersion in landscapes is typical of human migration and adaptation to geographical areas.

From the perspective of Earth, we can recognize Earth as a natural habitat that welcomes and enables peoples to create cultures in specific contexts. Cultures, as we know, are not created by the mastery of humans over nature in a given location, but by the interdependence of human and natural environments. Earth creates cultures as much as humans do. As we read, we are therefore conscious of Earth as a force in the creation of these peoples. It is Earth and Earth's domains—rather than God—who are involved in creating culture in Genesis 10.

d. *Genesis 10.6-14: The Legend of Ham*
The legend of Ham consists of a genealogy (Gen. 10.6-7, 13-14), a warrior legend (Gen. 10.8-9), and a story about the origin of great cities (Gen. 10.10-12).

Again, many of the progeny listed in this genealogy refer to nations mentioned elsewhere in the Bible. As some of these are linked to poignant memories—oppression in Egypt (Gen. 10.6); Canaan, the promised land (Gen. 10.6); Babylon, the land of exile (Gen. 10.10)—the genealogy is linked to geography and history, and to places where the Israelites experienced deep and meaningful attachments to domains of Earth.

The legend of Nimrod highlights the interest of the narrator in human achievements as distinct from natural wonders. The narrator represents those humans who, in line with the mandate to dominate in Gen. 1.26-28, are capable of great exploits, conquer animals or humans, and construct great cities. Nimrod's exploits are so memorable that in Israelite memory he is designated a 'mighty hunter before Yhwh'. Von Rad, however, claims that in this context the idiom 'before the Lord' means the same as 'on the Earth' (1961: 142; cf. Jon. 3.3). Unlike Cain, the first human to build a city, Nimrod does not seem to have left the presence of the Lord in achieving his goals (cf. Gen. 2.16-17). Though Nimrod's achievements correspond to those who build the Tower of Babel (Genesis 11), his achievements are not challenged by God.

e. *Genesis 10.15-20: The Legend of Canaan as Host*
The legend of Canaan consists of his genealogical connection with Ham (Gen. 10.15, 20), the peoples who are descended from Canaan (Gen. 10.16-18), and territories with Canaanite connections (Gen. 10.19).

Significantly, the legend of Ham (who saw the nakedness of his father, Noah) and of Canaan his son (cursed to be the lowest of slaves: Gen. 9.20-25), is not recalled here as a memory of what happens 'after the flood'. Yet, for most interpreters, the curse placed on Noah's grandson Canaan makes it difficult to empathize with Canaan, the land. It is difficult to be neutral with the tradition of Noah's drunkenness and Canaan's curse ringing in our ears. And for me, as an Australian, there is my knowledge of the heritage of early settlers who believe that the Indigenous Australian peoples, like the people of Canaan, have lost the image of God, are cursed like animals, and apparently are destined to be slaves.

> It was not simply that 'like the Hittites, and the Jebusites and the Aboriginal Canaanites, they had been left to the natural consequences of not retaining the knowledge of God' but that of all people in that condition, the Aborigines were judged to be on 'the lowest scale of degraded humanity' (Harris 1990: 30).

Yet the Genesis 10 tradition offers a very different perspective; it gives an alternative portrait of peoples, cultures and nations expanding across Earth without necessarily being in conflict or subordinating other peoples. Throughout this genealogy of Ham, Canaan is not cursed but is portrayed as an ancestor whose progeny also seems to spread across particular domains of Earth as part of a natural process of selection. For Canaan, 'after the flood' means moving into new territories and developing distinctive cultures.

According to Cassuto (1964: 209), the

> purpose of this list is not to tell us that a racial kinship existed between the peoples and tribes enumerated therein, but only to indicate the inhabitants of the country called in the Torah the land of Canaan, and thereby define the boundaries of the land that was assigned to the children of Israel.

The peoples and locations incorporated in the legend of Canaan, however, need not be viewed simply as denoting the boundaries of a land yet to be invaded by the Israelites. The fact that the land of Canaan included peoples of non-Canaanite origin suggests Canaan is a land where other peoples are welcome. Canaan is a host to more than those traditionally called 'Canaanites'. This role anticipates the Abraham legend in which the land functions as a host to the visiting family of Abraham. This ideology of land as host country—associated with Canaan in the Abraham narrative— is distinguishable from a range of other land ideologies elsewhere in the Hebrew Scripture (see Habel 1995, chapter 7).

As host country, Canaan here has a positive image as an open and diverse territory. In Genesis 10 there is no hint of pollution by false deities or other impediments. This land welcomes Abraham; this land is the third party in the covenant between Abraham and Abimelech (Gen. 21.22-23); this land becomes a fertile part of Earth 'after the flood' (Habel 2010).

In short, Canaan is a land of promise for several peoples in this text, not just for one!

We may also ask whether the narrator implies that God was active in Canaan long before the Israelites, the 'people of God', invaded the land— even if God is not mentioned in Genesis 10. If so, this legend suggests that God created a fertile land for various peoples to enjoy—Canaan is a habitat, created by God, for diverse peoples and cultures to develop.

f. *Genesis 10.21-31: The Legend of Shem*

The legend of Shem consists of a genealogy (Gen. 10.21-29), a description of the territories where the progeny live (Gen. 10.30), and a summary statement of their locations, languages and peoples (Gen. 10.31)

The genealogy of Shem is basically a listing of names that have been explored by scholars elsewhere. One enigmatic reference appears in Gen.

10.25 where it is said that when Eber gave birth to two sons, one was named Peleg, 'for in his days Earth was divided'. While the name Peleg may be a word play on the verb *plg*, to divide, there is clearly some cryptic tradition associated with Earth that belongs to the legend, whether it be an earthquake or some historical event. Given Genesis 10 gives an alternate portrayal of the dispersal of peoples on Earth, it is unlikely that this is an allusion to the divisions arising from the Tower of Babel legend. Whatever the allusion, there is a range of ancient traditions other than the Babel scenario about Earth and what happens to Earth after the flood.

g. Summation (Genesis 10.32): The Spread of Toledoth across Earth Post-Flood
The closing verse summarizes the spread of Noah's descendants across Earth after the flood. As Hamilton (1990: 346) points out, geographically the list extends as far east as Persia (Elam); as far south as Ethiopia (Cush) and the Arabian peninsula; as far north as Anatolia (Gomer, Madai); as far west as Crete (Kittim, Caphtorim) and Lybia. This range of lands and peoples represents Earth after the flood. This expanse of Earth is the habitat and the source of life for these peoples. Von Rad (1961: 156-58) offers a plausible portrait of the historical background to the peoples and nations outlined in Genesis 10. However, Genesis 10, in focusing on the geographical world that emerges after the flood, pays little attention to history.

This summation recognizes all these peoples and nations as descendants of Noah. Their dispersion across Earth, however, is not viewed as a direct result of a divine plan or course of action. In Genesis 10, God is not identified as a determining factor in the geography of Earth after the flood. Nor is there any indication in this sequence of legends that Israel is anticipated—even if the land and peoples of Canaan are part of this ancient geography. Rather, the focus is on Earth after the flood and how Earth has become the home for diverse peoples to enjoy, providing domains where diverse languages and cultures develop.

If indeed, Earth could have been designated *terra nullius* immediately after the flood when the family of Noah emerges from the ark, at the conclusion of the chapter Earth is clearly characterized as inhabited by a great range of diverse peoples. All these peoples apparently have a right to their domains. For subsequent generations to declare domains of Earth *terra nullius* negates the natural process of migration and settlement that seems to be articulated in this chapter. Wherever peoples settled they developed cultures in partnership with the domain of Earth where they lived. Earth as habitat extends to peoples the hand of hospitality, the capacity to create culture in partnership, and an invitation for mutual recognition of rights and service.

h. *Tower of Babel Legend (Genesis 11.1-9)*

Recent postcolonial studies reveal that the Tower of Babel narrative has a significant role as a resistance narrative among indigenous peoples. Against the background of a *terra nullius* mindset among invading nations and a popular belief that civilization and land ownership came with Europeans and especially European missionaries, the legend of the Tower of Babel provides an alternative message for indigenous peoples.

Mark Brett notes in *Decolonizing God* (2008: 34) that there is

> no suggestion in the primordial time of Genesis 1–11 that a particular culture can claim superiority. On the contrary, the whole point of the Tower of Babel story is that this attempt to grasp the high cultural ground, with a 'tower reaching up to the heavens' (11.4), is delusory and against God's intentions. No culture is represented as having divine favour, and when the people are dispersed they are shaped into a diversity of languages and cultures.

The Rainbow Spirit Elders (2007: 37), a group of Australian Indigenous leaders from Queensland, maintain that some

> Christian Aboriginal people point to the story of the Tower of Babel as further biblical support for our belief that the culture and land of Australia are God-given. The story in Genesis ends with people being given different languages and moving off in different directions as a result of God's intervention. Language is a bearer of all culture; the Aboriginal languages are no less bearers of culture than the languages of other lands.

The Tower of Babel legend is cited as a resistance narrative against those who claim mastery of land and language, country and culture. We may well ask whether the character of Earth, over whom humans seek to claim mastery in the light of the mandate to dominate in Gen. 1.26-28, also plays a role in this text. While no culture may claim superiority over another in this text, is Earth a partner to be shared equally by all cultures that the domains of Earth help to create? Earth is a welcome host and habitat for all peoples to share not to conquer.

1. *Setting (Genesis 11.1-2): All Earth One Language.* The setting for this legend announces from the outset that this story is about 'all of Earth' (*Erets*). The people on Earth, in this primordial context, have one language. The story is set after the genealogy of Shem (Gen. 10.21-31), and hence located after the flood. The announcement of a common language is in direct antithesis to the legends and summation of Genesis 10. The Babel narrative represents a radically different tradition to that elaborated in Genesis 10—a tradition that many scholars assign to the so-called Yahwist writer.

The movement of the people represents a typical migration; no reason is given for the move. Nor is there any special significance, it would seem, in the location chosen. This is a story about a migrating people who, upon reaching a new land, are inspired to reach new heights. It is interesting that there is apparently no parallel to this legend in other ancient Near Eastern literature, even though the setting of the story is in Mesopotamia and may reflect a satire on the great architectural achievements of Babylon (Cassuto 1964: 228-29).

The way the text is worded, Earth and the people are identified as one. That the whole Earth is said to have one language suggests that Earth is an integral part of the story. It is as if the whole Earth does the migrating. Upon arrival in Shinar, however, the focus is on the people involved. Earth then becomes the wider context with domains where different peoples may emigrate from, a context from which the people seek to escape.

The story as such, however, remains very anthropocentric and the scattering across Earth is viewed by the people of Earth as undesirable.

2. *Catalyst (Genesis 11.3-4): Humans Reaching for the Sky.* The catalyst for the plot of the story is reported as having several escalating stages: the making of bricks; the building of a city; the erection of a tower reaching the skies; the desire to become famous; the fear of being scattered across Earth.

In a domain where stone is not readily available for construction, the making of bricks to replace stone represents a willingness to achieve greatness even without the normal building materials. The produce of Earth is a natural resource for building a city. By building a city the people in Shinar follow the tradition of Cain—but in contrast to Cain, they do not seem to sever their connection with Yhwh as a consequence (see Gen. 4.16-17).

The term *shamayim* need not refer to heaven as the abode of God— the term may simply refer to the skies (as in Gen. 1.8). Nevertheless, the implication is that this building will be an expression of great human achievement and power.

Although there are no specific literary allusions to Genesis 1, the would-be heroes of this passage seem to be extending their role on Earth beyond the mandate to 'subdue Earth' in Gen. 1.28. They no longer want to spread across the face of Earth, but to centralize their efforts and focus them upwards. They are intent on 'conquering space', much like space heroes in modern human cultures. By mastering the skies above, they will achieve a fame that is unprecedented.

The ultimate ground for their ambitious design, however, is a rejection of Earth as their habitat. From the perspective of Earth, this is a rejection of their mother: the Earth that is the very source of their being. These humans, with a mindset of superiority, are seeking their place in the skies—

not on Earth where they belong. In the eyes of Earth, these human beings are fulfilling the very essence of the mandate to dominate that is imposed on Earth in Gen. 1.26-28. As the plot of this legend develops, there is a sense that this mandate to dominate is exposed as false by a tradition alien to the so-called Priestly perspective of Gen. 1.26-28.

Most commentators ignore this dimension of the text and highlight the great human achievements of this emerging people. Von Rad (1961: 144) speaks of the vital optimism of a young nation involved in a gigantic work of civilization: the city is a sign of their self-reliance, their mastery and their joy in their inventiveness. This great human achievement, however, betrays, as von Rad asserts, 'a concealed Titanism' or, in contextual terms, an unwarranted compulsion to subdue (1961: 144).

3. *Response (Genesis 11. 5-8): Divine Intervention.* The divine response to humanity's decision to build Babel is articulated in three stages: the descent of God to investigate the tower; an analysis of what is happening on Earth; a divine decision to intervene; and the act of intervention.

There may be a hint of irony in the narrator's portrait of God leaving the sky to visit Babel. From a celestial perspective, the tower may have been so tiny that a trip to Earth was needed to confirm God's suspicions. The narrator, however, immediately assumes the voice of Yhwh and articulates his analysis of the situation in bold speech. The *bene adam*, the descendants of the first humans, present a threat which demands action.

The action of humanity is presumably not a direct threat against God in the sky. Rather, these humans, with one language and one aggressive culture, are apparently capable of achievements that are either not part of the divine design for humans or not healthy for human existence. Excessive ambition is considered dangerous for human development on Earth...and ultimately with Earth.

There is also a touch of irony in the idiom 'nothing they propose (*zamam*) to do will now be impossible (*batsar*)'. Job (42.2) uses a variation of this idiom when speaking of God declaring that 'no purpose (*mezimma*) of yours will be thwarted (*batsar*)'. The image of humanity at Babel presented by the narrator suggests not only arrogant mortals sporting 'the image of God' but also creatures aspiring to invade God's realm.

Perhaps the supreme irony of this narrative, however, is an anticipation of the realization that as sons of *adam* they are also sons of *Adamah*: they are both human beings and Earth beings. In spite of their aspirations, they are destined to return to Earth—and the Babel legend guarantees just that. The Earth beings are brought down to Earth!

The divine response is not a punishment or angry retaliation, but rather a strategy to put humans in their place. This first involves a rather humorous scenario in which the Babel construction workers, despite their grand urban ambitions, are all talking to each other in different tongues. There is a confused babble in Babel, reflecting a popular etymology of the name Babel—from *balal* 'to confuse'. The world of potential skyscrapers in Shinar is reduced to a ludicrous scene devoid of effective communication.

The decision of Yhwh is executed and construction work comes to an end. The urban dream is demolished. The people scatter over 'the face of all the Earth'. For Cain, the face of *Adamah* was associated with the presence of Yhwh (Gen. 4.14). Now the face of Earth represents the diverse domains where the dispersing peoples find diverse habitats suitable for creating new cultures. These are diverse Earth-connected cultures rather than a sky-oriented urban monoculture. All domains of Earth are host to the diverse peoples of Earth.

4. *Closure (Genesis 11. 9: Dispersal across Earth.* The closure of this myth re-announces that Yhwh executes a decision to confuse the common language and scatter the people across the face of Earth. The popular etymology for the meaning of Babel is made explicit, after the event. It is explicitly 'from there', from the central location of Babel, that humanity spreads to become the diverse cultures on Earth. The context may suggest 'after the flood' as its beginning; the scene closes with a transformed world that emerges 'after Babel'!

i. *The Origins of Culture: Three Traditions.*There appear to be at least three biblical traditions that explore the origin of cultures, each with a rather different orientation and appreciation of the physical domain on Earth that contributes to a given culture.

Genesis 10 focuses on the natural migration of peoples after the flood. In this tradition, the various domains of Earth become the habitats for a diversity of cultures. Canaan, for example, becomes the host for a range of cultures, including the Jebusites and Amorites. In Genesis 10, God does not intervene or govern the locations of a given people: country and community combine to create culture; land and language unite to identify a given people. In a given habitat a specific culture evolves. The locus and culture of Israel is not identified.

In Genesis 11, the creation of cultures is initiated by God in response to the desire of humanity to become one culture governed by arrogant urban ambitions. Peoples with their diverse languages are then scattered across Earth. In various domains and in diverse locations of Earth, diverse cultures with diverse languages evolve. Earth, which is initially deserted by humanity, provides habitats for numerous cultures to evolve. The locus and culture of Israel is not identified.

In Deut. 32.8-9, we find a third tradition according to which Elyon, the most high God, functions as a celestial administrator and map-maker. Humanity is divided into nations, rather than tongues, and each nation is then assigned a territory on Earth marked by specific boundaries. The remarkable emphasis in this text is that the criterion for fixing these territories is the specific deity of a given location. In this tradition, culture is linked, first and foremost, to the local deity rather than the physical domain of a nation. In this context, the portion allocated to Yhwh, the God of Israel, is not a territory but a people. Israel is initially a people without a land, en route to a land where another culture has emerged. Prior to Israel residing in any fixed physical habitat or location, Yhwh is portrayed as the source of Israel's culture.

By contrast, Deuteronomy 7 portrays Canaan as a land with a range of cultures that have no right to be present. Their gods are polluting powers rather than local deities appropriate to their domains. These cultures must therefore be cleared from their host country. In their place, a new ecosystem is anticipated in which fertility is dependent on direct divine intervention in response to rigid observance of divine ordinances. Though this passage suggests a fourth tradition, in Genesis the origin of the Israelite culture is viewed as different from the origin of these other cultures.

If we identify with Canaan, we realize just how differently peoples of Earth have viewed the land that bears his name. Canaan is viewed as a welcoming host, a fertile habitat, a *terra nullius*, a polluted landscape. Canaan, a land of promise for any who respect her hospitality, is viewed as a polluted land by those who invade under the leadership of Joshua.

1. *Genesis 11.10-26: The Legend of Shem.* Genesis 11.10-26 provides a more detailed genealogy for Shem than the version reported in Gen. 10.21-31. The significant difference lies in the focus on the human family line, ignoring any association with the geographical territories or languages typical of the other legends in Genesis 10–11. The Genesis 11 version is exclusively anthropocentric; the Genesis 10 version is conscious of country and culture. Details relating to the individuals named in this genealogy have been explicated by numerous exegetes.

2. *Genesis 11.27-32: The Legend of Terah.* The legend of Terah is specifically constructed to introduce the figure of Abram and the land of Canaan. More personal details are given about the families of Terah's children: Haran, Nahor, Abram. Haran's son is Lot, a future character in the Abram legends. Nahor's wife is Milcah. Abram's wife is Sarai who happens to be barren. In general the orientation is anthropocentric and androcentric.

The crucial factor in this legend is Terah's decision of to migrate with Abram, Sarai and Lot to the 'land of Canaan'. Such migrations may well have been relatively common in this period. The specific motivation for Terah's migration to Canaan is not recorded, nor are there any indications why Canaan is perceived to be desirable country in which to make a new beginning. There is also no indication that Terah is motivated by a divine impulse or religious experience. The fact that the family settled in Haran, a location en route to Canaan, suggests that escaping Ur of the Chaldees is more important than a specific geographical destiny. No description is given about conditions in the Chaldees. The Hurrian communities of Haran may well have initially influenced the culture of the patriarchs. Their welcome in Canaan by their Canaanite hosts, however, is probably decisive in the evolution of the patriarchal culture.

Though the social conditions are not recorded, this version of the Terah legend recognizes that the geographical factor is integral to the formation of the people who remember Abram as their ancestor.

3. Retrieval

In the history of interpreting Genesis, the colourful account known as the Tower of Babel in Genesis 11 has had priority over the more prosaic legends of Genesis 10. The links in Genesis 10 and 11 between genealogy and geography, and between language and location, have been ignored. If, however, we now identify with Canaan—a key location in the legends of Genesis 10–11—we can retrieve an ecological voice that is rarely heard. This is the suppressed voice of Canaan, host to a diversity of peoples long before it is designated a promised land for God's people Israel.

The Voice of Canaan
I am Canaan, the land of Canaan. I was named after the grandson of Noah, the hero of the flood.

The flood! What a cruel and crushing experience! As the waters rose, my face was slowly submerged. As the waters rose, the children I had nurtured faced death and extinction. As the waters rose, more and more forms of life disappeared. It was unbelievably distressing. I groaned with anger and empathy.

At first, animals and insects in the valleys were drowned. Then the hills were covered with water and almost all my children suffocated and died. All the plants, flowers and trees lost their leaves—and their lives—beneath the waters. Even the birds, with no place to land, sank into the waters. Soon the surface was covered with death and debris.

I lay beneath those waters with my bloated children floating above me. It was horrible. Soon I suffocated in my watery tomb.

After the flood! After the flood, I was born anew. After the flood, I emerged from beneath the waters, appearing as Earth did in the very beginning. After the flood, the landscape was regenerated. I again brought forth all forms of life from within my soil: insects, grasses, trees, flowers. Dormant seeds erupted and life began again. It was amazing!

I am Canaan, a small territory on Earth. I do, however, have a range of domains where life developed in various ways. I have coastal regions where coastal communities emerged. I have valleys where agricultural societies evolved. I have semi-arid areas where pastoral pursuits are possible. And

I have wildernesses where semi-nomadic peoples live in harmony with creatures from the kingdom of the wild.

In each of these areas I provide a habitat for a culture to evolve: humans interacting collaboratively with the environment that I provide. After the flood, I have been home to many cultures—Jebusites, Amorites, Hivites, and more.

Communities on the coast had a sense of divine presence in the ocean, a presence they called Yam. Cultures in the fertile valleys had a sense of divine presence in the fertile forces of the ecosystems I provided; they called these forces Baal and Anat. And a community of Jebusites on a central mountain, later called Zion, experienced the divine presence as a creator, a high god called El Elyon.

I was home to all of these cultures from the new beginning I experienced after the flood.

I also welcomed peoples from other cultures travelling through my lands from the great Nile River to the south, and to the great rivers of Mesopotamia in the east. I also welcomed immigrants who believed their deity wanted me to be their home. I hosted immigrants from Ur of the Chaldees who chose to migrate from the east and settle on my soil. The first of these were descendants of Shem, a family headed by Abram and Sarai.

There is a popular story that all humanity converged on one location in Mesopotamia and began to build a tower. The peoples dreamed of an urban edifice that would storm the skies. God intervened, however, and relocated these peoples across Earth, each with its own language and emerging culture. I can assure you, however, that from the beginning I provided the habitat and environment for peoples to develop their worldview and cultural orientation. I did not need a Babel to initiate a context for creating cultures!

From the beginning I was the host, home and habitat for all these peoples with their diverse tongues and tastes. I hoped that each of them would see me as such and live on my domains in harmony with each other, with the land, and with the living creatures that inhabit my domains after the flood.

APPENDICES

1. *The Adamah Myth*

Adamah *and her Caretaker*, adam
In the beginning *Adamah* was barren, devoid of vegetation, rain or a caretaker. A spring rose from *Adamah* and flowed across the landscape.

Y<small>HWH</small> Elohim took some of the soil of *Adamah* and moulded a figure
called *adam*. Y<small>HWH</small> Elohim then blew some of his breath into the nostrils of
adam and it became a living being.

The primordial domain where this happened was called Eden. In Eden,
Yhwh Elohim planted on *Adamah* a forest with trees of great beauty and
trees with fruit to eat. He also planted the tree of life and the tree of the
knowledge of good and bad.

From the river that watered the forest, four tributaries flowed out of Eden
into the wider world. These rivers were called Pishon, Gihon, Tigris, and
Euphrates.

Yhwh Elohim then took *adam* and placed *adam* in the forest of *Adamah*
to be its caretaker, to 'serve and preserve' it; *adam* was forbidden to eat of
the tree of knowledge—if *adam* did *adam* would face death.

Since *adam* was alone, Yhwh Elohim decided to find a partner for *adam*.
So from *Adamah*, Yhwh Elohim formed a range of animals and birds. Yhwh
brought them to *adam* who gave them all names. But none of them was
quite suitable to be *adam*'s personal partner.

So Yhwh Elohim caused *adam* to fall asleep, took one of its ribs, made a
woman and brought her to *adam*, who said: 'At last, someone with my flesh
and bones'.

Though the man *adam* and his partner were naked, they knew no shame.

How Adamah *Was Cursed*
Now the snake was wiser than all the other creatures Yhwh Elohim had
made. The snake asked the woman whether God had really said they could
not eat from any tree in the forest. She replied that God had said they
could eat of any tree except the tree in middle of the forest, or touch it, or
otherwise they would die.

The snake then corrected the woman and told her she would not really
die. Rather, if she ate of that tree she would be enlightened, and be like
God, knowing about good and bad.

Then the woman saw the fruit of the tree was not only good for food but a chance to become wise. So she ate some and shared some with her partner. They were both enlightened and realized they were naked. So they sewed some fig leaves together to serve as loincloths.

Later, when the man and the woman heard Yhwh Elohim walking in the forest and enjoying the evening breeze, they hid themselves among the trees. When Yhwh Elohim called out, 'Where are you?', the man *adam* replied, 'I heard your sound in the forest and I was afraid, because I was naked. So I hid myself.'

Yhwh Elohim replied, 'Who said you were naked? Did you eat from the tree I commanded you not to eat from?' And *adam* replied, 'That woman you gave me, she gave me fruit from the tree and I ate'. Then Yhwh Elohim said to the woman, 'What have you done, woman?' The woman replied, 'The snake tricked me and I ate'.

Then Yhwh Elohim pronounced several curses. He declared the snake the most cursed of all animals, condemned to crawl on its belly, eat dust, and live at enmity with the progeny of the woman.

He declared that the woman would experience pain in childbirth and suffer the indignity of being ruled by her partner, *adam*.

Then God also cursed *Adamah*, forcing her to bring forth thorns and thistles that would make it arduous for the man *adam* when he tried to cultivate her soil. His life would be characterized by sweat and toil until he returned home to *Adamah* from whom he originated.

Recognizing her as the mother of all living, *adam* named his partner Eve. Then Yhwh Elohim made garments from animal skins to cover their nakedness.

Yhwh Elohim conferred with his council and admitted that the humans had become 'like one of us, knowing about good and bad'. So, to prevent them living in the forest of Eden and also eating from the tree of life, Yhwh Elohim sent them out of the forest of Eden to be caretakers of *Adamah* from which the man *adam* was taken. To guarantee they could not return to Eden, Yhwh Elohim posted celestial guardians to protect the way to the tree of life.

Why Cain Left Adamah

The first humans, the man *adam* and his wife Eve, had two sons: Cain and Abel. Eve believed that her first son was her special creation—with some help from Yhwh.

Abel was a keeper of sheep and Cain a tiller of *Adamah*. In time Cain brought some of the produce of *Adamah* as an offering to Yhwh and Abel brought the best of the firstlings of his flock.

For no apparent reason, Yhwh regarded the offering of Abel favourably but paid not regard to the offering of Cain. That made Cain angry. Yhwh confronted Cain and asked him why he was angry; Yhwh challenged him to do the right thing and not let sin lurk like a wild animal at his door: he should master it rather than let it seduce him.

Cain went with his brother into a field of *Adamah*. There, Cain killed his brother Abel.

Yhwh then put Cain on trial and interrogated him. 'Where is your brother Abel?' Cain replied, 'I don't know. Am I supposed to be my brother's keeper?' Yhwh continued, 'The blood of your brother is crying out from *Adamah*; *Adamah* has testified against you! My verdict is that you are to be cursed from *Adamah*; when you try to till *Adamah* it will not yield any produce.'

Cain protested that his punishment was too harsh. To be driven from *Adamah* meant being driven from the very presence of Yhwh and to be at risk of being killed. So Yhwh placed a mark on Cain to protect him from potential murderers.

Cain then left *Adamah* and the presence of Yhwh, and settled far away in the land of Nod.

How Rainwater Covered Adamah

After *adam* multiplied on *Adamah*, they became progressively sinful, thinking evil thoughts continuously. Yhwh regretted having made *adam* and decided to blot out every *adam*. Yhwh, however, went a step further and decided to blot out all things living on the face of *Adamah*. One person called Noah found favour in the eyes of Yhwh.

Yhwh informed Noah about an imminent flood and told him to take seven of every clean species into a boat and two of every unclean species so that their seed could be perpetuated in the future. Yhwh shut Noah and his entourage up in the boat. It then rained for 40 days and 40 nights until water covered the face of *Adamah* and killed all life on *Adamah*.

When the rain ceased Noah opened a window and sent out a raven, but it did not return. After seven days, he sent out a dove, but it returned because the dove could not find a resting place among the waters. After another seven days, he sent out another dove and it returned with an olive branch. Noah waited yet another seven days and sent out the dove once more. But this time the dove did not return. So Noah removed the canopy covering his boat and behold the face of *Adamah* was dry.

When the Curse Was Removed from Adamah

When Noah emerged from his boat, he built an altar and offered a massive burnt offering using one of every clean animal and bird. When Yhwh smelled the aroma, he decided to remove the curse on *Adamah* so that it would be as fertile as it was in the beginning. Yhwh also realized that *adam* had not really changed: *adam* was still thinking bad thoughts and so Yhwh would have to live with the situation; but Yhwh decided never again to destroy all life on *Adamah*.

Yhwh also assured *adam* that the climate would be stable; the seasons and times of seedtime and harvest, cold and heat, summer and winter, day and night would never cease.

2. *The* Erets *Myth*

Birth of Erets

In the beginning *Erets* was located in the primordial waters, a cosmic domain called the Deep. In that primordial womb, *Erets* was present, like an embryo, as yet unformed and without signs of life. Above those waters, the wind of God hovered, like a midwife. The primordial cosmos was in total darkness.

First, God separated the darkness by creating light and thereby illuminated the primordial cosmos. Even before she emerged from the cosmic waters, *Erets* could then be seen below the surface of the Deep.

Second, God separated the cosmic waters by constructing a dome, so that some of the cosmic waters were above the dome and some were below. That dome was called *shamayim* or Sky. And *Erets* was still located in the cosmic waters below the dome.

Then came the big day! God separated the cosmic waters below the dome and they parted, like the bursting waters of a womb. Next God summoned the solid land mass beneath the waters to appear. Immediately there was a geophany—an appearance from beneath the waters: and the solid land mass was born. God named the newborn solid land mass *Erets*, looked at her and said, 'She's fantastic!'

Soon God invited *Erets* to demonstrate she was alive and fertile by producing all kinds of flora that possessed seeds and could perpetuate their species on *Erets*; *Erets* obliged and flora emerged from across her entire body. And *Erets* became green.

God also placed lights in the sky above to illuminate *Erets* below, to order her seasons, and to separate night from day. God then invited the waters below the sky to swarm with life and for birds to fly above *Erets* in the sky. God also blessed these creatures so that they could multiply on *Erets*.

Finally, God invited *Erets* to give birth to all kinds of living creatures: wild animals and reptiles, camels and cattle. God looked at what *Erets* produced and said, 'That's fantastic!'

God told all the creatures of *Erets* that the vegetation produced by *Erets* was food for their sustenance. God took a final look at what had been created and said, 'Absolutely fantastic'.

At last God rested and *Erets* nurtured all life. God separated the seventh day of the week as a sacred day for rest and the rejuvenation of life on *Erets*.

The Corruption of Erets
When the various living species, known as all flesh, multiplied on *Erets*, they began to change. They no longer lived according to the 'way' implanted in them by Elohim. Their lawlessness meant that *Erets* was filled with chaos instead of natural order. Only one human, called Noah, was doing the right thing and 'walking with Elohim'. So Elohim decided to destroy all life on *Erets* and *Erets* as well.

The Destruction of Erets
Elohim decided to destroy all life by means of a flood. However, Elohim made a covenant with Noah to keep him, his family and two of every species of living beings alive. To achieve this Elohim gave Noah directions on how to construct a boat that would house a male and female of every species, along with enough food to survive. Noah built the boat as Elohim directed him and the representative species boarded the boat.

Then there was a cosmic upheaval. The fountains of the cosmic deep erupted and the windows in the sky opened. Cosmic waters from above and below inundated *Erets* until not even a mountain tip could be seen; *Erets* was buried deep in the primordial cosmic waters again.

This cosmic upheaval lasted for over 12 months. After 150 days, Elohim send a wind to begin blowing back the cosmic waters. When *Erets* was finally dry, Elohim told Noah to release all species of life from the boat so that they could multiply on *Erets* as *Erets* had come to life again.

A Covenant with Erets
After the flood Elohim told Noah that Elohim was establishing a covenant with all living creatures—all *basar*—and promising there would never again be a flood of cosmic waters that would destroy all *basar* or *Erets*.

As a witness to this covenant, Elohim put a rainbow in the sky and designated it a sign of the covenant between Elohim and *Erets*. Elohim promised that whenever he saw that rainbow, he would remember his covenant with all flesh and *Erets*.

3. The tselem Myth

In the beginning, Elohim viewed creation and saw there was no creature on *Erets* that looked like Elohim and so could represent Elohim. So God convened a meeting of the council of *elohim* beings and announced a plan to make a new species that would look like Elohim. They would embody the very *tselem* of Elohim and could therefore represent Elohim on *Erets*.

After creating this new species, Elohim separated them into male and female, blessed them and thereby imparted to them the capacity to multiply and completely fill *Erets*. Because these new beings, whom Elohim called humans, looked like Elohim and bore Elohim's distinctive *tselem*, they would immediately be identified as Elohim's representatives. They were then given the mandate to be Elohim's representatives, ruling over all other living creatures and subduing *Erets*. Their *tselem* was the guarantee of their imparted power to rule *Erets* and subdue her powers.

When the human species began to procreate and fill *Erets*, they perpetuated the *tselem* of Elohim: all the parents and their children looked like Elohim. Humans multiplied until the days of a righteous man called Noah.

After the flood, Elohim blessed Noah so that his and his wife's progeny could multiply and fill *Erets* once again. He announced again that humans still have the right to rule other living creatures, all of whom are given into human hands to control. As a result they would be terrified of humans.

Elohim also gave humans the right to eat their animal kin but not to drink their blood because blood is their source of life from Elohim. The killing of humans was also forbidden, because they bear the *tselem* of Elohim. Humans after the flood still bear the *tselem* of Elohim, represent Elohim on *Erets*, and dominate all other living creatures.

BIBLIOGRAPHY

Anderson, A.A., 1972, *The Book of Psalms*, II (Greenwood: Attic Press).

Anderson, Bernhard, 1994, *From Creation to New Creation* (Minneapolis: Fortress Press).

Barr, James, 1968, 'The Image of God in the Book of Genesis—A Study of Terminology', *BJRL* 51, pp. 11-26.

Berry, Thomas, 1999, *The Great Work: Our Way into the Future* (New York: Bell Tower).

Birch, Charles, 1990, *On Purpose* (Sydney: University of New South Wales Press).

Boomershine, Thomas, 1980, 'Structure and Narrative Rhetoric in Genesis 2–3', in *Genesis 2 and 3: Kaleidoscopic Structural Readings* (ed. Daniel Patte; Semeia 18; Chico, CA: SBL), pp. 113-30.

Brett, Mark, 2008, *Decolonizing God: The Bible in the Tides of Empire* (Sheffield: Sheffield Phoenix Press).

Brueggemann, Walter, 2002, *The Land* (Philadelphia: Fortress Press).

—1982, *Genesis. Interpretation: A Commentary for Teaching and Preaching* (Atlanta: John Knox Press).

Cassuto, U., 1964, *A Commentary on the Book of Genesis*, II (Jerusalem: Magnes Press).

Clines, David J.A., 1979, 'The Significance of the "Sons of God" Episode (Genesis 6.1–4) in the Context of the "Primeval History" (Genesis 1–11)', *JSOT* 13, pp. 33-46; reprinted in *On the Way to the Postmodern: Old Testament Essays, 1967–98*, I (JSOTSup, 292; Sheffield: Sheffield Academic Press), pp. 337-50.

Code, Lorraine, 2006, *Ecological Thinking: The Politics of Epistemic Location* (Oxford: Oxford University Press).

Conradie, Ernst M., 2004, 'Toward an Ecological Biblical Hermeneutics: A Review Essay of the Earth Bible Project', *Scriptura* 85, pp. 123-35.

Devashayam, V., 1992, *Outside the Camp: Bible Studies from a Dalit Perspective* (Madras: Gurukul Lutheran Theological College).

Deane-Drummond, C., 1996, *A Handbook in Theology and Ecology* (London: SCM Press).

Dryness, William, 1985, 'Stewardship of the Earth in the Old Testament', in W. Granberg-Michaelson (ed.), *Tending the Garden: Essays on the Gospel and the Earth* (Grand Rapids: Eerdmanns), pp. 50-65.

Dundes, Alan (ed.), 1988, *The Flood Myth* (Los Angeles: University of California Press).

Earth Bible Team, 2001, 'The Voice of Earth: More Than Metaphor?', in Norman Habel (ed.) *The Earth Story in the Psalms and the Prophets* (The Earth Bible, 4; Sheffield: Sheffield Academic Press), pp. 23-28.

Eaton, Heather, 1996, 'Ecological-Feminist Theology: Contributions and Challenges', in Dieter Hessel (ed.), *Theology for Earth Community: A Field Guide* (Maryknoll, NY: Orbis Books), pp. 77-92.

—2000, 'Ecofeminist Contributions to an Ecojustice Hermeneutics', in Habel (ed.) *Readings from the Perspective of Earth* (The Earth Bible, 1; Sheffield: Sheffield Academic Press), pp. 54-71.

Edwards, Denis, 2006, *Ecology at the Heart of Faith: The Change of Heart That Leads to a New Way of Living on Earth* (Maryknoll, NY: Orbis Books).

Fejo, Wally, 2000, 'The Voice of Earth: An Indigenous Reading of Genesis 9', in Norman Habel and Shirley Wurst (eds.), *The Earth Story in Genesis* (The Earth Bible, 2; Sheffield: Sheffield Academic Press), pp. 140-46.

Fergusson, David, 1998, *The Cosmos and the Creator: An Introduction to the Theology of Creation* (London: SPCK).

Friedman, Thomas, 2006, *Hot, Flat and Crowded: Why We Need a Green Revolution and How It Can Renew America* (New York: Farrar, Straus & Giroux).

Frymer-Kensky, Tikva, 1988, 'The Atrahasis Myth and its Significance for our Understanding of Genesis 1–9', in Alan Dundes (ed.), *The Flood Myth* (Berkeley: University of California Press), pp. 61-74.

Gardner, Anne, 2000, 'Ecojustice: A Study of Genesis 6.11-13', in Norman Habel and Shirley Wurst (eds.), *The Earth Story in Genesis* (The Earth Bible, 2; Sheffield: Sheffield Academic Press), pp. 50-65.

Garr, Randall, 2001, *In his Own Image and Likeness: Humanity, Divinity and Monotheism* (Leiden: E.J. Brill).

Goodenough, Ursula, 1998, *The Sacred Depths of Nature* (Oxford: Oxford University Press).

Green Bible, The, 2008 (San Francisco: HarperCollins).

Gunkel, Hermann, 1997, *Genesis* (trans. Mark E. Biddie; Georgia: Mercer University Press).

—2006, *Creation and Chaos in the Primeval Era and the Eschaton: A Religio-Historical Study of Genesis 1 and Revelation 12* (trans. K. William Whitney; Grand Rapids: Eerdmans).

Gunn, David, and Diana Fewell (eds.), 1993, *Narrative in the Hebrew Bible* (Oxford: Oxford University Press).

Habel, Norman C., 1971, *Literary Criticism of the Old Testament* (Philadelphia: Fortress Press).

—1972, 'He Who Stretches out the Heavens', *CBQ* 34, pp. 417-30.

—1988, 'The Two Flood Stories in Genesis', in Alan Dundes (ed.), *The Flood Myth* (Berkeley: University of California Press), pp. 13-28.

—1993, 'The Sacred Story: Myth', in Norman Habel, Michael O'Donohue and Marion Maddox (eds.), *Myth, Ritual and the Sacred* (Adelaide: University of South Australia), pp. 41-44.

—1995, *The Land Is Mine: Six Biblical Land Ideologies* (Minneapolis: Fortress Press).

—2000a, 'The Challenge of Ecojustice Readings for Christian Theology', *Pacifica* 13, pp. 125-41.

—2000b, 'Geophany: The Earth Story in Genesis 1', in Norman Habel and Shirley Wurst (eds.), *The Earth Story in Genesis* (The Earth Bible, 2; Sheffield: Sheffield Academic Press), pp. 34-48.

—2000c, 'Guiding Ecojustice Principles', in Habel (ed.), *Readings from the Perspective of Earth* (The Earth Bible, 1; Sheffield: Sheffield Academic Press), pp. 38-53.

—2000d, 'Introducing the Earth Bible', in Habel (ed.) *Readings from the Perspective of Earth* (The Earth Bible, 1; Sheffield: Sheffield Academic Press), pp. 25-37.

—2001, 'Is the Wild Ass Willing to Serve You? Challenging the Mandate to Dominate', in Norman Habel and Shirley Wurst (eds.), *The Earth Story in Wisdom Traditions* (The Earth Bible, 3; Sheffield: Sheffield Academic Press), pp. 179-89.

—2003a, 'The Origins and Challenges of an Ecojustice Hermeneutic', in Timothy Sandoval and Carleen Mandolfo (eds.), *Relating to the Text: Interdisciplinary and Form-Critical Insights on the Bible* (Edinburgh: T. & T. Clark), pp. 141-59.

—2003b, 'The Implications of God Discovering Wisdom in Earth', in Ellen van Wolde (ed.), *Job 28: Cognition in Context* (Leiden: E.J. Brill), pp. 281-98.

—2006a, 'What Kind of God Would Destroy Earth Anyway? An Ecojustice Reading of the Flood Narrative', in Wesley Bergen and Armin Siedlecki (eds.), in *Voyages in Unchartered Waters: Essays in Theory and Practice of Biblical Interpretation in Honor of David Jobling* (Sheffield: Sheffield Phoenix Press), pp. 203-11.

—2006b, 'Playing God or Playing Earth? An Ecological Reading of Genesis 1.26-28', in Frederick Gaiser and Mark Throntveit (eds.), *And God Saw That It Was Good: Essays on Creation and God in Honor of Terence Fretheim* (WWSup, 5; St Paul, MN: Luther Seminary), pp. 33-41.

—2007, 'The Beginning of Violence: An Ecological Reading of Genesis 4', in John O'Grady and Peter Scherle (eds.), *Ecumenics from the Rim: Explorations in Honour of John D'Arcy May* (London: Transaction Publishers), pp. 79-86.

—2008b, 'Introducing Ecological Hermeneutics', in Habel and Trudinger (eds.), *Exploring Ecological Hermeneutics* (SBL Symposium, 20; Atlanta: SBL), pp. 1-8.

—2009, *An Inconvenient Text: Is a Green Reading of the Bible Possible?* (Adelaide: ATF Press).

—2010, 'Canaan—Land of Promise: An Ecological Reading of Gen. 10.15-10 in Context', in Frank Ritchel Ames and Charles William Miller (eds.), *Foster BIblical Scholarship: Essays in Honor of Kent Harold Richards* (Atlanta: SBL).

Habel, Norman C., (ed.), 2000e, *Readings from the Perspective of Earth* (Earth Bible, 1; Sheffield: Sheffield Academic Press).

Habel, Norman, and Peter Trudinger (eds.), 2008a, *Exploring Ecological Hermeneutics* (SBL Symposium, 20; Atlanta: SBL).

Harris, Michael, 1990, *One Blood: 200 Years of Aboriginal Encounter with Christianity; A Story of Hope* (Sydney: Albatross Books).

Hamilton, Victor, 1990, *The Book of Genesis, 1–17* (NICOT; Grand Rapids: Eerdmans).

Hiebert, Theodore, 1996, *The Yahwist's Landscape: Nature and Religion in Early Israel* (Oxford: Oxford University Press).

—2008, 'Air, the First Sacred Thing: The Conception of *Ruach* in the Hebrew Scriptures', in Habel and Trudinger (eds.), *Exploring Ecological Hermeneutics* (SBL Symposium, 20; Atlanta: SBL), pp. 9-19.

Hillel, Daniel, 2006, *The Natural History of the Bible: An Environmental Exploration of the Hebrew Scriptures* (New York: Columbia University Press).

Howard, Cameron, 2008, 'Animal Speech as Revelation in Genesis 3 and Numbers 22', in Habel and Trudinger (eds.), *Exploring Ecological Hermeneutics* (SBL Symposium, 20; Atlanta: SBL), pp. 21-30.

Jenson, Robert, 2006, *The Rough Guide to Climate Change* (London: Roughguides).

Kahl, Brigitte, 2001, 'Fratricide and Ecocide: Re-reading Genesis 2–4', in Dieter Hessel and Larry Rasmussen (eds.), *Earth Habitat: Ecojustice and the Church's Response* (Minneapolis: Fortress Press), pp. 53-70).

Kikawada, Isaac, 1975, 'The Shape of Genesis 11.1–9', in Jared Jackson and Martin Kessler (eds.), *Rhetorical Criticism: Essays in Honor of James Muilenburg* (Pittsburgh: Pickwick), pp. 18-32.

Lacocque, André, 2006, *The Trial of Innocence: Adam, Eve and the Yahwist* (Eugene, OR: Cascade Books).

Lemche, Niels Peter, 1991, *The Canaanites and their Land: The Tradition of the Canaanites* (JSOTSup, 110; Sheffield: JSOT Press).

Lovelock, James, 2006, *The Revenge of Gaia* (London: Allen Lane).

Luther, Martin, 1958, *Genesis*, I (ed. Jaroslav Pelikan; St Louis: Concordia Publishing House).

Macy, Joanna, and John Seed, 1996, 'Gaia Meditations', in Roger S. Gottlieb (ed.), *This Sacred Earth: Religion, Nature and Environment* (New York: Routledge), pp. 501-502.

Marlow, Hilary, 2008, 'The Other Prophet! The Voice of Earth in the Book of Amos', in Habel and Trudinger (eds.), *Exploring Ecological Hermeneutics* (SBL Symposium, 20; Atlanta: SBL), pp. 75-84.

Meadowcraft, Tim, 2006, *Haggai* (Readings: A New Biblical Commentary; Sheffield: Sheffield Phoenix Press).

McBride, S. Dean, 2000, 'Divine Protocol: Genesis 1.1–2.3 as Prologue to the Pentateuch', in S. Dean McBride, Jr, and William P. Brown (eds.), *God Who Creates* (Grand Rapids: Eerdmans), pp. 3-41.

Middleton, Richard, 2005, *The Liberating Image: The* Imago Dei *in Genesis 1* (Grand Rapids: Brazos).

Miller, Patrick M., 1972, 'In the Image and Likeness of God', *JBL* 91, pp. 289-304.

Moltmann, Jürgen, 1985, *God in Creation: An Ecological Doctrine of Creation* (London: SCM Press).

Newsom, Carol, 2000, 'Common Ground: An Ecological Reading of Genesis 2–3', in Norman Habel and Shirley Wurst (eds.), *The Earth Story in Genesis* (The Earth Bible, 2; Sheffield: Sheffield Academic Press), pp. 60-73.

Northcott, Michael, 2007, *A Moral Climate: The Ethics of Global Warming* (London: Darton, Longman & Todd).

Olley, John, 2000, 'Mixed Blessings for Animals: The Contrasts of Genesis 9', in Norman Habel and Shirley Wurst (eds.), *The Earth Story in Genesis* (The Earth Bible, 2; Sheffield: Sheffield Academic Press), pp. 130-39.

Orlinsky, Harry, 2001, 'The Biblical Concept of the Land of Israel: Cornerstone of the Covenant between God and Israel', in L.A. Hoffman (ed.) *The Land of Israel: Jewish Perspectives* (Notre Dame: University of Notre Dame Press).

Pardes, Ilana, 1992, *Countertraditions in the Bible: A Feminist Approach* (Cambridge, MA: Harvard University Press).

Petersen, David, 1979, 'Genesis 6.1–4: Yahweh and the Organization of the Cosmos', *JSOT* 13, pp. 47-64.

Pietrantonio, Ricardo, 1995, 'God Is Sole Creator and Lord', in *Concern for Creation* (Uppsala: Tro & Tanke).

Plumwood, Val, 1993, *Feminism and the Mastery of Nature* (New York: Routledge).

Ponting, Clive, 1991, *A Green History of the World: The Environment and the Collapse of Great Civilisations* (London: Penguin).

Rad, Gerhard von, 1961, *Genesis: A Commentary* (Philadelphia: Westminster).

Raheb, Mitri, 2006, 'Land, People and Identities: A Palestinian Perspective' (2006 *Charles Strong Trust Lecture*; see www.charlesstrongtrust.org.au under 'Lectures').

Rainbow Spirit Elders, 1997; repr. 2007, *Rainbow Spirit Theology: Towards an Australian Aboriginal Theology* (Melbourne: HarperCollins).

Renner, J.T.E., 1988, *Genesis* (Adelaide: Lutheran Publishing House).

Römer, Thomas Christian, 2006, 'The Elusive Yahwist: A Short History of Research', in Thomas Dozeman and Konrad Schmid (eds.), *Farewell to the Yahwist? The Composition of the Pentateuch in Recent European Research* (SBL Symposium, 34; Atlanta: SBL), pp. 9-28.

Schottroff, Louise, 1993, 'The Creation Narrative: Genesis 1.1–2.4a', in Athalya Brenner (ed.), *A Feminist Companion to Genesis* (Sheffield: Sheffield Academic Press), pp. 24-38.

Schungel-Straumann, H., 1993, 'On the Creation of Man and Woman in Genesis 1–3: The History and Reception of the Texts Considered', in Athalya Brenner (ed.), *A Feminist Companion to the Bible*, I (Sheffield: Sheffield Academic Press).

Schüssler Fiorenza, Elizabeth, 1985, 'The Will to Choose or to Reject: Continuing our Critical Work', in Letty Russell (ed.), *Feminist Interpretation of the Bible* (Philadelphia: Westminster Press), pp. 125-36.

Speiser, E.A., 1964, *Genesis* (The Anchor Bible; New York: Doubleday).

Swenson, Kristin, 2008, 'Earth Tells the Story of Cain', in Habel and Trudinger (eds.), *Exploring Ecological Hermeneutics* (SBL Symposium, 20; Atlanta: SBL), pp. 31-40.

The Green Bible—*see Green Bible, The*

Towner, W. Sibley, 2005, 'Clones of God: Genesis 1.26-28 and the Image of God in the Hebrew Bible', *Interpretation* 59, pp. 341-57.

Tsumura, David, 2005, *Creation and Destruction: A Reappraisal of the Chaoskampf Theory in the Old Testament* (Winona Lake, IN: Eisenbrauns).

Vawter, Bruce, 1956, *A Path through Genesis* (New York: Sheed & Ward).

Wallace, Howard, 2000, 'Rest for Earth? Another Look at Genesis 2.1-3', in Habel (ed.), *Readings from the Perspective of Earth* (The Earth Bible, 1; Sheffield: Sheffield Academic Press), pp. 49-59.

Westermann, Claus, 1964, *The Genesis Accounts of Creation* (Philadelphia: Fortress Press).

Williams, Jay, 1981, 'Expository Articles—Genesis 3', *Interpretation* 35, pp. 274-79.

Wittenberg, Gunther, 2000, 'Alienation and Emancipation from the Earth', in Norman Habel and Shirley Wurst (eds.), *The Earth Story in Genesis* (The Earth Bible, 2; Sheffield: Sheffield Academic Press), pp. 105-16.

Wolde, Ellen van, 1998, 'Facing the Earth: Primaeval History in a New Perspective', in P.R. Davies and D.J.A. Clines (eds.), *The World of Genesis: Persons, Places, Perspectives* (JSOTSup, 257; Sheffield: Sheffield Academic Press), pp. 22-47.

—1991, 'The Story of Cain and Abel: A Narrative Study', *JSOT* 52, pp. 25-41.

—2009, 'Why the Verb *Bara'* Does Not Mean "To Create" in Genesis 1.1–2.41', *JSOT* 34.1, pp. 3-23.

Wurst, Shirley, 2000, '"Beloved Come Back to Me": Ground's Theme Song in Genesis 3', in Norman Habel and Shirley Wurst (eds.), *The Earth Story in Genesis* (The Earth Bible, 2; Sheffield: Sheffield Academic Press), pp. 87-104.